Lion House Classics

SHADOW
MOUNTAIN

Design and photo art direction by Shauna Gibby. Photography by Alan Blakely. Food styling by Maxine Bramwell.

© 2004 Temple Square Hospitality Corporation

Visit us at shadowmountain.com

Library of Congress Cataloging-in-Publication Data

Lion House classics.
     p. cm.
 Includes index.
 ISBN 1-59038-354-0 (hardback : alk. paper)
 1. Cookery, American. I. Lion House (Restaurant)
 TX715.L75938 2004
 641.5973—dc22

                          2004011835

Printed in the United States of America
Quad Commercial & Specialty

10   9   8

42316

Contents

Children's Party Room and Lion House Taffy

Introduction

It is with great pleasure that the Lion House management and staff bring you the 25th anniversary edition of the original Lion House cookbook.

The Lion House, nestled in the heart of downtown Salt Lake City, was built in 1856. The house is named for the stone statue of a reclining lion on the portico above the front entrance. The charm and warmth of the past remains ever present today.

The Lion House was originally the family residence for Brigham Young, colonizer, territorial governor, and second president of The Church of Jesus Christ of Latter-day Saints. It is now a popular gathering place for wedding banquets and receptions, business meetings, family dinners, children's birthday parties, and other special occasions.

The ground level of the house was originally used as the family's food storage area, weaving room, and laundry room. A schoolroom was located in the northwest corner. After a schoolhouse was completed in 1862, the room became the family's recreation room, complete with a stage and large hooks on the walls for pulling taffy. A long dining room ran along the southwest side of the house, where the family, workers, and guests ate supper each evening. It is now the site of the Lion House Pantry, where hot meals and delicious bakery items are served to the public daily.

The main floor consisted of a parlor where the evening meeting and family prayer were held. The original bell Brigham Young used to call his family together is displayed in the wall across from the parlor. The remaining rooms on the main floor were used as bedrooms for the families with small children. Today this floor is used for smaller banquets and wedding receptions. The rooms have been decorated in keeping with the original style of the time. The Garden Room leads to the outside garden area, where wedding receptions are held on summer evenings.

The upper floor originally housed twenty small bedrooms. Each dormer window represents a bedroom, ten on each side of the long hallway. The original interior walls have been removed, and the area can now be used for banquets in three large dining rooms. The dividers can also be opened to accommodate a wedding reception.

The Lion House is a favorite place for children to celebrate their birthdays. The party guests are greeted by a hostess. After a short tour of the house, the guests enter the children's party room where they can dress up in bonnets or coonskin caps. Pioneer stories are told and pioneer games are played.

One highlight of the party is the taffy pull. Each child receives a piece of warm taffy and is instructed on how to stretch and pull it until it turns white. The hostess teaches the song that was sung by Brigham's children while they enjoyed the same type of activity.

Lion House Taffy

2	cups sugar
1½	cups water
1	cup white corn syrup
1	teaspoon salt
2	teaspoons glycerine (available at drugstores)
2	tablespoons butter
1	teaspoon vanilla

Mix sugar, water, corn syrup, salt, and glycerine in a heavy saucepan. Bring to a boil and cook until temperature is 258 degrees. Remove from heat and add the butter and vanilla, stirring until the butter is melted. Pour candy onto a buttered cookie sheet. Cool until lukewarm and taffy can be handled comfortably. Wash and dry hands thoroughly. Take a small piece of taffy and stretch and fold repeatedly until the taffy turns white. Form taffy into desired shape. Place on a piece of waxed paper. Makes enough taffy for 10 to 14 people to share.

The Taffy Pull Song

Come to the taffy pull, come one and all.
Come to the taffy pull, come hear our call.
Pull on the candy warm, pull with all your might.
But don't take a bite, until it turns white!

Refreshments at a birthday party consist of ribbon sandwiches, carrots, a nut cup, and punch. The birthday guest of honor is then presented with a beautifully decorated cake, personalized by our Lion House bakers. One lucky guest may find the surprise that is hidden in the cake—a gumball for good luck!

At the conclusion of the party, each guest receives a ginger cookie, a favorite of Brigham's children. The birthday child then receives a special pioneer birthday packet containing twelve raisins, sunflower seeds, and sugar cubes, and is instructed to eat one raisin a month counting down to his or her next birthday. A special gift from the Lion House is also given to the birthday child.

Ginger Cookies

½	cup granulated sugar
½	cup brown sugar
¾	cup shortening
¼	cup molasses
1	egg
2	cups all-purpose flour
2	teaspoons soda
¼	teaspoon salt
1	teaspoon cinnamon
1½	teaspoons ginger

Preheat oven to 350 degrees. In a large mixing bowl, combine sugars and shortening until mixture is light and fluffy. Add molasses and egg; beat well. Add flour, soda, salt, cinnamon, and ginger and beat well. Scrape down the sides of bowl; then mix again. Drop dough by rounded tablespoonfuls onto a lightly greased cookie sheet. Press down each cookie with the bottom of a glass dipped in sugar. Bake for 8 to 10 minutes, being careful not to overbake. Makes approximately 2½ dozen cookies.

Acknowledgments

We would like to thank the many people involved in bringing together the twenty-fifth anniversary edition of the original Lion House cookbook. Many hours were spent on testing and retesting both the old and the new recipes, on the photography, and on the food styling and design.

A special thanks to the following Lion House employees who made this all possible:

Julie Ulrich, Brenda Hopkin and the bakery staff, Ann Sudweeks, Alba Marroquin, David Bench, Leonel Perez, Julie Gardner, Barbara Carling, Jenny Barlow, and Neil Wilkenson.

Thanks also to the many people at Deseret Book: Jana Erickson, Jay Parry, Lisa Mangum, Shauna Gibby, and Tonya Facemyer.

We also express thanks to Maxine Bramwell for her expertise in food styling and Alan Blakely for the beautiful photography.

Special thanks to the following businesses and individuals for loaning us dishes and linens for the photos: The Basket Loft, Gentler Times, Meier & Frank, Mervyn's, Pier One, Target, Jana Erickson, Sarah Gibby, Shauna Gibby, Geri Hallows, Russell Nielsen, and Kerry Reed.

We hope the recipes become as treasured in your home as they are in ours.

The Lion House Staff

Children's Birthday Party Cake

Ribbon Sandwiches

Lion House Cheese Ball

- 1 package (8 ounces) cream cheese, softened
- 1½ cups grated Cheddar cheese
- 1 tablespoon dried chives
- 2 teaspoons dry ranch dressing mix
- ½ cup chopped pecans

Mix all ingredients together. Form into a ball and roll in chopped pecans. Serve with assorted crackers.

Party Roll-Ups

- 12 thin slices white bread
- 8 slices bacon, cooked, drained, and crumbled
- 2 packages (3 ounces each) cream cheese, softened
- 12 spears asparagus, cooked and cooled
  Melted butter

Trim crusts from slices of bread; roll with rolling pin to flatten slightly. Blend bacon bits with cream cheese and spread mixture on bread slices. Lay one cooled asparagus spear on each slice of bread and roll up. Place on baking sheet, seam side down. Cover and refrigerate until serving time. Brush with melted butter and toast at 350 degrees until lightly browned, about 15 to 18 minutes. Serve hot. Makes 12 appetizers.

Ribbon Sandwiches

- 2 loaves bread, sliced in three horizontal layers each (may be ordered through most bakeries; ask for ribbon sandwich bread)
- 1 recipe Cream Cheese Filling (below)
  Mayonnaise
- 1 recipe Chicken Salad Filling (below)
  Paprika
  Parsley flakes

Spread half of Cream Cheese Filling on bottom layer of horizontally sliced bread loaf. Add next layer of bread; spread with small amount of mayonnaise. Cover layer with half of Chicken Salad Filling. Add last layer of bread, spreading top and bottom with mayonnaise. If desired, sprinkle top with paprika and dry parsley flakes. Repeat with second loaf and other half of filling ingredients. Trim crusts on all four sides. Slice each loaf vertically into 12 ribbon sandwiches. Makes about 24 sandwiches.

Note: Fillings will spread much easier if frozen sliced bread is used.

Cream Cheese Filling

- 1 package (8 ounces) cream cheese, softened
- 1¼ cups crushed pineapple, drained slightly
- ¼ cup sugar

Combine all ingredients and mix well.

Chicken Salad Filling

- 4 cups cooked chicken, shredded
- 1 cup celery, finely minced
- ⅓ cup yellow onion, finely minced
- ½ teaspoon salt
- 1 cup mayonnaise
  Pepper to taste

Combine all ingredients and stir until well blended.

Lion House Birthday Ribbon Sandwiches

Filling for one loaf, following the directions for Ribbon Sandwiches:

Bottom layer—½ cup Cheese Whiz

Top layer—1 can (6 ounces) tuna, mixed with ¼ cup mayonnaise

Sassy Slush

1   cup sugar
1   cup water
1   can (18 ounces) grapefruit juice
1   cup orange juice
2   tablespoons lemon juice

Bring sugar and water to a hard boil; cool. Add other ingredients. In bowl or ice-cube tray, freeze mixture until slushy. Makes 8 servings.

Sassy Slush and Cranberry Nut Bread

Stuffed Mushrooms

Stuffed Mushrooms

50   medium-sized fresh mushrooms
½   pound country-style sausage
1   package (8 ounces) cream cheese
3   tablespoons fresh parsley, chopped
¾   teaspoon garlic powder
      Salt and pepper to taste

Wash and remove stems from mushrooms. Combine uncooked sausage, cream cheese, parsley, garlic powder, salt, and pepper. Roll stuffing into small balls and fill mushroom caps. Cover and bake at 400 degrees for about 30 minutes. Drain drippings and serve hot.

Spinach Dip

Spinach Dip

1 package (10 ounces) frozen spinach
½ cup sour cream
¾ teaspoon salt
⅛ teaspoon white pepper
⅛ teaspoon onion juice, *or* finely chopped onion
⅛ teaspoon Worcestershire sauce
4 drops hot sauce

Cook spinach according to package directions; drain. Place in strainer or colander and run cold water over to keep the color green. Squeeze or mash until all water is removed and spinach is very dry. Place spinach in blender and chop well. Add enough sour cream to moisten to dip consistency. Add remaining ingredients and blend just until combined. Adjust seasonings to taste. Chill before serving.

Hot Spinach Dip

1 package (10 ounces) frozen creamed spinach, thawed
1 package (8 ounces) cream cheese
¼ cup mayonnaise
2 tablespoons chopped green onion
9 tablespoons grated Parmesan cheese

Mix all ingredients except half the Parmesan cheese. Spread in 9x9-inch pan, and sprinkle other half of Parmesan on top. Bake at 350 degrees for 25 minutes. Serve with chips or crackers.

Fiesta Sausage Dip

1 pound ground country sausage
2 cans (10 ounces each) diced tomatoes with green chilies
2 packages (8 ounces each) cream cheese

Brown and rinse sausage. Add tomatoes with chilies and bring to a boil. When boiling, add cream cheese and stir. Serve warm with bread, crackers, or chips.

Hot Zippity Tomato Dill Drink

1 can (46 ounces) tomato juice
4 tablespoons sugar
1 teaspoon salt
¼ teaspoon garlic salt
2 tablespoons Worcestershire sauce
3 drops Tabasco® sauce
½ cup dill pickle juice
⅓ cup lemon juice

Combine all ingredients in saucepan. Bring mixture to a boil. Let stand to develop flavors. Adjust seasonings to taste. Serve hot or cold. Garnish with chopped chives or dollop of sour cream, if desired. Makes 7 cups, about 12 servings.

Fruit Salsa

1 can (15½ ounces) crushed pineapple, drained
2 cans (11 ounces each) mandarin oranges, drained and chopped
2 bunches green onions, chopped
2 small jalapeno peppers, diced
1 bunch cilantro, chopped

Drain crushed pineapple and mandarin oranges. In large bowl, mix pineapple, oranges, green onions, jalapenos, and cilantro. Serve with tortilla chips.

Tomato Drink

1 can (46 ounces) tomato juice
1 can (46 ounces) vegetable juice cocktail
2 cans (10½ ounces each) consommé, undiluted
1 can (10½ ounces) tomato soup
1 soup can water
  Seasoned salt, celery salt, onion salt
1 cup heavy cream, unsweetened and whipped

Heat juices, consommé, soup, water, and seasonings to a boil; strain and cool. When ready to serve, top with whipped cream. Serve either hot or cold. Makes about 4 quarts.

Tomato Tune Up

3	cups tomato juice
½	cup sliced celery
2	thin slices onion
1	bay leaf
4	whole cloves
2	dashes Tabasco sauce
1	cup beef broth
4	thin slices lemon, halved

In saucepan, combine tomato juice, celery, onion, bay leaf, and cloves. Bring to a boil and add Tabasco sauce. Reduce heat and cover; let simmer for 20 minutes. Strain soup, discarding seasonings. Return to saucepan and add broth. Bring to a second boil. Serve in soup bowls; float halved lemon slice in each bowl. Makes 4 one-cup servings.

Tomato Drink

Wassail

½   cup sugar
2   cups water
5   whole cloves
4   allspice berries
1   cinnamon stick
½   piece ginger root, approximately 2 inches
2   cups orange juice
1   cup lemon juice
1   quart apple cider or juice

Combine sugar and water. Boil 2 minutes, then remove from heat and add spices. Cover and allow to stand in warm place for 1 hour. Strain; add juices and cider. Bring quickly to a boil. Remove from heat and serve at once. Makes about 8 cups.

Ice Cream Apricot Nectar

1 cup chilled apricot nectar
2 teaspoons lemon juice
Pinch salt
1 tablespoon sugar
1 large scoop vanilla ice cream

Put apricot nectar into blender; add lemon juice, salt, and sugar. Add ice cream and blend until ice cream partially melts. Serve at once. Makes 2 cups.

Fruit Punch with Sherbet

2 cans (46 ounces each) pineapple-grapefruit juice
1 can (6 ounces) frozen lemon juice
1 can (6 ounces) frozen lime juice
2 juice cans water
Pinch salt
1 quart lime sherbet
2 quarts ginger ale

Mix fruit juices, water, and salt. Let stand overnight in refrigerator. Before serving, add lime sherbet and ginger ale. Makes 30 punch-cup servings.

Banana Freeze

4 cups sugar
6 cups water
5 oranges
2 lemons
5 bananas
1 quart apricot or pineapple juice
Lemon-lime carbonated beverage

Boil sugar and water 3 to 5 minutes, until sugar is well dissolved; cool. Squeeze juice from oranges and lemons; mash bananas. Combine orange and lemon juices, mashed bananas, and apricot or pineapple juice. Add to sugar and water mixture and freeze. When ready to serve, chop frozen mixture and spoon into sherbet dishes or punch cups and pour lemon-lime carbonated beverage over. Makes 12 to 16 servings.

Fruit Freeze

4 cans (16 ounces each) grapefruit segments, undrained
1 can (11 ounces) mandarin oranges, undrained
½ cup sugar
1 small jar maraschino cherries, undrained
Juice from ½ lemon
2 cans (20 ounces each) crushed pineapple, undrained
1 bottle (12 ounces) lemon-lime carbonated beverage
1 pint lime sherbet

Whirl grapefruit, oranges, and sugar together in blender for about 30 seconds. Chop cherries; add cherries, cherry juice, lemon juice, and crushed pineapple to blended fruits. Pour into freezer trays or loaf pans and freeze. When ready to serve, chop frozen mixture and spoon into serving cups. Pour lemon-lime beverage over and top with small scoop of sherbet. Makes 15 to 20 punch-cup servings.

Three-Fruit Slush

1 cup sugar
2 cups water
2 cups (4 to 6) mashed bananas
½ cup fresh lemon juice
1 can (6 ounces) frozen lemonade
1 can (6 ounces) frozen orange juice
3 juice cans water

Combine sugar and 2 cups water. Boil about 3 minutes, then cool. Mash bananas; combine fruit juices and water; add bananas to fruit juices and sugar syrup. Pour into pans; freeze until slushy, stirring occasionally. If desired, remove slush from pan and beat with egg beater once during freezing. Serve plain or pour ginger ale or similar carbonated beverage over slush just before serving. Makes about 20 punch-cup servings.

Fruit Freeze

Lemon Water

1	gallon water
2	tablespoons citric acid
2	tablespoons pure lemon extract
2 to 3	cups sugar

or

5	gallons water
10	tablespoons citric acid (⅔ cup less 2 tablespoons)
10	tablespoons pure lemon extract (⅔ cup less 2 tablespoons)
10 to 12	cups sugar

Lion House Tomato Bisque

Soups

Brown Soup Stock

1 or 2	marrow bones, cracked
4	pounds beef shin, cut in small pieces
3	quarts cold water
⅓	cup each chopped celery, carrots, onion, white turnips
2	sprigs parsley, chopped
5	whole cloves
8 to 10	peppercorns
1	bay leaf
¼	teaspoon each marjoram and thyme
1	tablespoon salt

Scrape marrow from bones; melt in kettle over moderate heat. Brown about half the beef in marrow fat. Add remaining beef, bones, and water; cover and slowly bring to a boil. Remove scum. Add vegetables and seasonings; cover and simmer gently about 4 hours, removing scum occasionally. Strain, chill, remove fat, and strain again. Use for soups and sauces. Makes about 2 quarts stock.

Note: Vegetables and seasonings may be varied as desired. For added flavor, vegetables may be simmered in butter for 10 minutes before adding to soup.

Chicken Stock

4	pounds chicken, quartered or cut in pieces
	Chicken giblets (optional)
	Cold water
1	teaspoon salt
4	ribs celery, cut in 3-inch pieces
3	carrots, cut in 3-inch pieces
1	medium onion, with whole clove inserted in each end
1	large leek, sliced (optional)
¼	cup fresh chopped parsley

Place chicken and giblets in large saucepan. Cover with cold water; add salt. Slowly bring to a boil and simmer until chicken is almost tender. Remove scum from surface as it forms. Add celery, carrots, onion, and leek. Simmer until chicken is fork tender. Remove from heat. Add parsley and let stand 30 minutes.

Place cheesecloth in strainer. Remove chicken from pan; strain stock through cheesecloth. Remove strainer. Skim off fat as it rises to top of stock. (This is easier to do with fat-skimming whisk, or if stock is chilled.) Stock can be frozen and used when needed. Cooked chicken may be used in a variety of creamed dishes. Remove skin and bones and cut meat in cubes. Meat may also be frozen for later use.

Vegetable Soup

1	cup diced tomatoes
1½	cups diced carrots
1	cup diced celery
1½	quarts water
¼	cup chopped onion
1	tablespoon beef soup base, *or* beef consommé
½	cup green beans
1	cup diced potatoes
½	pound cooked beef, cut in pieces
1	cup peas

Cook together tomatoes, carrots, celery, water, onion, and beef soup base until carrots and celery are tender. Add green beans, potatoes, beef, and an additional cup of water. Simmer until vegetables are tender. Add peas about 5 minutes before serving. Adjust seasonings to taste. Makes 3 quarts, about 12 one-cup servings.

Lion House Tomato Bisque

12 to 15	Roma tomatoes
4	cans (10½ ounces each) tomato soup
2	cups chicken stock
1	cup beef stock, or canned beef consommé
1	bunch fresh basil, or 2 tablespoons dry basil
1	cup sugar
2 to 3	cups cream
	Salt and pepper

Roast tomatoes in oven at 350 degrees until tops begin to blacken. In large pot combine tomato soup, chicken stock, and beef stock. Place roasted tomatoes and basil in blender and puree until smooth. (Cover blender with the lid and a towel to avoid splashing when hot tomatoes puree.) Add puree to pot and let simmer. Add sugar until mixture is slightly sweet (don't skimp on the sugar—it may take more or less, depending on the tomatoes), then add cream. Season to taste with salt and pepper.

Note: The soup should not taste like marinara sauce, but should have a slightly sweet creamy flavor.

Mongolian Hot Pot

½	pound bacon, diced
1	pound lean ground beef, or 2 cups diced cooked ham
1	can (10½ ounces) condensed beef broth, or 3 teaspoons beef soup base
1	quart water
1	onion, chopped
1	green pepper, chopped
1	carrot, sliced
1	tablespoon soy sauce
1	can (16 ounces) tomatoes
1	package (10 ounces) frozen mixed vegetables
1	zucchini, sliced
2	teaspoons salt
⅛	teaspoon pepper
1	tablespoon finely chopped parsley (optional)

Fry bacon in large, heavy saucepan until crisp. Pour off all but 2 tablespoons bacon fat. Drain bacon on absorbent paper. Sauté beef or ham in the 2 tablespoons bacon fat. Add next seven ingredients and simmer gently for about 1 hour. Add mixed vegetables and zucchini, and simmer another 10 minutes. Add salt and pepper. Adjust seasonings to taste. Add chopped parsley just before serving. Makes about 10 cups, or 10 one-cup servings.

Roux

Mix 2 cups flour and 1 cup butter or margarine, melted, together until well blended. Store in refrigerator. When ready to use, add a little at a time to gently boiling liquid. Stir constantly until preferred consistency is reached.

Note: The Lion House uses roux to thicken soups. The amount used depends upon individual taste.

Minestrone

1	cup navy beans
½	pound diced bacon
⅓	pound diced ham
½	cup chopped onion
2	cups beef stock
1½	cups canned tomatoes
1½	cups chopped carrots
1	cup green beans
1	cup chopped cabbage
1	cup chopped celery
1	cup spaghetti, broken into pieces
	Salt and pepper

Soak beans overnight in water to cover. Boil beans in soaking water until tender, about 2 hours; add more water as needed. Cook bacon until crisp; drain, and crumble. Sauté ham and onion in bacon fat. To beans, add beef stock, bacon, ham, and onion, then tomatoes, carrots, green beans, cabbage, celery, and spaghetti. Cook until fresh vegetables are tender, 10 to 15 minutes. Add salt and pepper to taste. Makes about 3 quarts, or 12 one-cup servings.

Carrot Apple Bisque

5 to 6	large carrots, peeled
1	tablespoon butter or margarine
	About 4 cups chicken broth
1	large apple, *or* ½ cup unsweetened applesauce
½	cup light cream
½	teaspoon nutmeg
⅓	cup minced green onion, including tops

Cut carrots into ½-inch chunks. Combine in saucepan with butter and 1 cup chicken broth. Cook, covered, until carrots are very tender, about 20 minutes. In the meantime, peel, core, and slice apple, adding it (or applesauce) to carrots for last 5 minutes of cooking. Remove pan from heat, uncover, and allow to cool for about 10 minutes.

Whirl carrot mixture in blender until smooth, or force mixture through strainer. Stir in light cream and nutmeg, then remaining chicken broth, until soup is desired consistency. Serve hot, or cover and refrigerate to serve cold. Sprinkle with chopped green onion. Makes 6 to 8 servings.

Gazpacho

1	clove garlic
4	ripe tomatoes, peeled and quartered
½	large green pepper, seeded and sliced
½	small onion, peeled and sliced
1	teaspoon salt
¼	teaspoon pepper
2	tablespoons olive oil
3	tablespoons vinegar
½	cup ice water

Using about half the ingredients at a time, fill blender container with vegetables; add seasonings, olive oil, vinegar, and water. Cover and blend for only 2 seconds. Repeat with other half of ingredients. Chill in refrigerator or pour into soup plates and serve with an ice cube in the center of each serving. Makes 6 servings.

Chicken and Corn Chowder

¼	cup chopped onion
2	tablespoons chopped green pepper
2	tablespoons butter or margarine
3	cups milk
1	can (10½ ounces) cream of chicken soup
1	can (12 or 16 ounces) corn niblets, undrained
1	teaspoon chicken base
¼	teaspoon salt

Cook onion and green pepper in butter until soft but not browned. Add remaining ingredients; simmer for about 5 minutes to develop flavor. For heartier soup, minced chicken may be added as desired. Thicken with a little roux, if desired. Makes 5 to 6 cups, about 6 servings.

Golden Squash Soup

1	small onion, sliced
2	tablespoons butter or margarine
¼	cup flour
5	cups milk
1½	cups winter squash (hubbard, banana, etc.), cooked and puréed
1½	teaspoons salt
¼	teaspoon celery salt
⅛	teaspoon curry powder
	Pepper to taste
2	tablespoons parsley, chopped

In large saucepan, cook onion in butter for a few minutes. Blend flour with onion; add milk. Cook over low heat, stirring constantly, until thickened. Remove from heat; gently blend in squash and seasonings. Heat to serving temperature but do not boil. Sprinkle each serving with parsley. Makes 6 one-cup servings.

Note: A 12-ounce package of frozen puréed squash may be used in this recipe. Add squash; continue to heat soup only until squash is defrosted.

Zucchini Soup

3 cups (about 1 pound) sliced zucchini
½ cup water
1 tablespoon fresh or instant minced onion
1 teaspoon seasoned salt
½ teaspoon parsley flakes, *or* 2 tablespoons
   chopped fresh parsley
2 teaspoons chicken soup base, *or*
   2 bouillon cubes
2 tablespoons butter or margarine
2 tablespoons flour
⅛ teaspoon white pepper
1 cup milk
½ cup light cream
Paprika
Sour cream

Combine zucchini, water, onion, seasoned salt, parsley, and 1 teaspoon soup base. Cook until zucchini is tender and most of water has evaporated. Mash or purée zucchini and set aside. In saucepan melt butter; blend in flour and rest of soup base and pepper. Add milk and cream, and simmer until thickened. Stir in puréed vegetables; thin with milk, if desired. Garnish with paprika and sour cream. Adjust seasonings to taste. Makes 4 to 6 servings.

California Chowder

California Chowder

¼ pound butter
1 cup flour
1 tablespoon chicken soup base
2 cups whipping cream
4 cups whole milk
4 cups water
2 cups diced carrots
4 cups diced potatoes
2 cups diced celery
1 teaspoon granulated garlic, *or* 2 cloves
   fresh minced garlic
1 tablespoon salt
1 tablespoon Worcestershire sauce
1 cup finely chopped onions
1 tablespoon vegetable oil
2 cups fresh broccoli
2 cups fresh cauliflower
   Fresh parsley for garnish

In a large soup pot, melt butter. Add flour and mix well. Add chicken base, whipping cream, whole milk, and water. Bring to a low boil; then add carrots, potatoes, celery, garlic, salt, and Worcestershire sauce. Cook for 45 minutes. Sauté onions in vegetable oil for 3 minutes and add to soup mix with broccoli and cauliflower. Cook another 15 minutes or until vegetables are tender. Makes 12 servings.

Macaroni and Tomato Soup

2 tablespoons butter or margarine
½ cup onion, chopped
¼ cup diced green pepper
1 cup diced celery
1 can (10½ ounces) tomato soup
1 can water
1 can (46 ounces) tomato juice
4 ounces macaroni, cooked
   Dash of pepper
½ teaspoon salt (or to taste)
½ teaspoon sweet basil
1 tablespoon sugar
1 to 2 bay leaves

In heavy saucepan, melt butter; cook onion, green pepper, and celery until limp but not brown. Add remaining ingredients. Heat to boiling. Makes 10 to 12 one-cup servings.

Spiced Tomato Soup

1 can (46 ounces) tomato juice
1 tablespoon sugar
1 tablespoon chicken soup base
3 cups water
2 tablespoons taco seasoning (or to taste)

Combine ingredients and bring to a boil. Adjust seasonings to taste. Serve hot or cold. Makes 8 to 10 servings.

Western Tomato Soup

3 slices bacon, cooked and crumbled
½ cup finely chopped celery
3 tablespoons finely chopped onion
¼ cup finely chopped green peppers
3 tablespoons flour
2 cups milk
1 can (10½ ounces) tomato soup
2 cups stewed tomatoes, *or* one 16-ounce
   can
1½ cups tomato juice
   Salt and pepper to taste

Sauté celery, onion, and green pepper in bacon fat until limp and transparent but not browned. Add flour and cook for 2 to 3 minutes. In 3-quart saucepan, combine milk and tomato soup; heat and stir until smooth. Combine all ingredients except bacon with tomato soup mixture. Heat and stir until slightly thickened. Garnish with crumbled bacon. Makes about 8 one-cup servings.

Crab Bisque

1 can (10½ ounces) each condensed cream
   of tomato, celery, mushroom, and green
   pea soups
5 cups milk (part cream, if desired)
1 or 2 cans crab meat
   Salt
   Pepper
   Parsley

Combine and blend soups. Heat milk; gradually add to soups, then add crab meat. Heat slowly, stirring constantly to prevent scorching. Season to taste; add chopped parsley. Makes 12 servings.

Corn Chowder

- 2 slices bacon, cooked and crumbled
- 1 small onion, chopped
- 1½ cups boiling water
- 1 package (16 ounces) frozen corn, *or* 1 can (15¼ ounces) corn, undrained
- ½ teaspoon salt
  Dash pepper
- 1¾ cup evaporated milk
- 1 tablespoon butter
- 1 tablespoon flour

Cook bacon slowly in large saucepan until crisp; remove and drain on paper towels. Add onion to pan and cook until transparent but not brown, about 20 minutes. Add boiling water, corn, seasonings, and milk. Blend butter and flour to make a roux. Stir into soup mixture; mix until smooth. Cook until thickened. Served topped with crumbled bacon. Makes about 4 servings.

Chicken Soup with Dumplings

- 1 large yellow onion, diced
- ½ stalk celery, diced
- 2 carrots, diced
  Meat from 1 chicken, cooked and shredded
- 4 to 6 cups chicken broth
- 1 cup fresh cut green beans
- 1 cup pearl barley (optional)
- 1 teaspoon celery salt
- 1 tablespoon fresh chopped parsley
- 2 bay leaves
- 1 teaspoon thyme
  Salt
  Pepper

In small amount of cooking oil, sweat onion, celery, and carrots. Add remaining ingredients and simmer until barley is tender or vegetables softened. Season to taste with salt and pepper. Add spoon-sized balls of dumpling dough (below) and simmer until dumplings rise.

Dumplings

- 1 cup milk
- ½ cup butter

- ½ teaspoon salt
- ½ teaspoon nutmeg
- 1 cup flour
- 3 eggs

Bring milk and butter to a boil; add salt and nutmeg. Remove from heat and immediately add flour, stirring until dough leaves sides of pan. Add eggs one at a time, forming a sticky dough.

Hearty Chicken Noodle Soup

- 2 teaspoons chicken soup base, *or* 2 bouillon cubes
- 3 cups canned chicken stock
- 2 cups chopped carrots
- 2 cups chopped celery
- ¾ cup chopped onion
- 2 cans (10½ ounces each) cream of chicken soup
- ¼ cup evaporated milk, *or* ½ cup whole milk
  Roux (see page 12)
- 2 cups cooked diced chicken
- 2½ ounces (about 4 cups) cooked noodles
  Salt and pepper to taste

Heat chicken soup base and stock together. Add carrots, celery, and onion, and simmer until vegetables are tender. Add cream of chicken soup and milk. Thicken with roux as desired, then add cooked chicken and noodles. Add salt and pepper to taste. Makes about 2½ quarts, or 10 one-cup servings.

Homemade Noodles

- 1 cup flour
- 1 teaspoon herb of choice (such as parsley, thyme, basil, oregano, or chives)
- 1 egg
  Water to bind

Combine herb and flour on work surface. Form a cone in flour and work egg into flour. Add water a spoonful at a time to make a firm yet workable dough. Roll out paper-thin; cut into strips.

Hearty Chicken Noodle Soup

Canadian Cheese Soup

Clam Chowder

¼	pound butter
⅓	cup ground onion
½	cup flour
⅓	cup cornstarch
1½	quarts half-and-half or milk
1¼	cups clam nectar
1	cup clams
1	cup diced potatoes, cooked
1	cup diced celery, cooked
1	teaspoon garlic salt
1	tablespoon Worcestershire sauce
1	teaspoon salt
½	teaspoon pepper

Melt butter in double boiler; add onion, and sauté. Add flour and cornstarch; cook 10 minutes. Add milk and clam nectar; cook until slightly thickened. Add clams and vegetables. Add garlic salt and Worcestershire sauce. Season to taste, and top with chopped parsley. Serves 6 to 8.

Canadian Cheese Soup

Ingredients	10 servings (2½ quarts)	60 servings (2½ gallons)
Chopped onion	½ cup	2 cups
Butter or margarine	½ cup	2 cups
Flour	1 cup	4 cups
Cornstarch	⅓ cup	1½ cups
Paprika	½ teaspoon	1½ teaspoons
Salt	½ teaspoon	2 teaspoons
White pepper	¼ teaspoon	1 teaspoon
Half-and-half or milk, heated	1 quart	1 gallon
Chicken stock, heated	1 quart	1 gallon
Diced carrots, cooked	¾ cup	3 cups
Diced celery, cooked	¾ cup	3 cups
Shredded sharp Cheddar cheese	1 cup	1 quart
Chopped parsley	¼ cup	¾ cup

Sauté onion in melted butter until transparent but not brown, 5 to 10 minutes. Add flour, cornstarch, paprika, salt, and pepper. Cook on low heat for about 10 minutes. Add half-and-half or milk and chicken stock; cook, stirring constantly, until thickened. Chop cooked vegetables very fine, or mash slightly; add to milk mixture. Adjust seasonings to taste. Just before serving, stir in shredded cheese and chopped parsley.

Note: Amount of vegetable may be increased if thicker soup is desired. Use 1 cup added vegetables in 10-serving recipe, 3½ to 4 cups in 60-serving recipe. (Servings are based on one-cup amounts.)

Chili

1	pound diced lean beef
1	green bell pepper, chopped
1	red bell pepper, chopped
1	medium yellow onion, chopped
1	teaspoon crushed red pepper flakes
1½	tablespoons chili powder
1	teaspoon granulated garlic, *or* 2 cloves fresh garlic, minced
1	teaspoon cumin
1	teaspoon crushed black pepper
1½	teaspoons kosher salt
½	teaspoon cayenne pepper
1	tablespoon canola oil
2	cans (8 ounces each) diced tomatoes
1	can (4 ounces) diced green chilies
4	cups canned kidney beans, rinsed and drained
2	cups tomato soup
1	cup tomato juice
1	cup brown sugar
	Sour cream
	Cheese, grated
	Onion, finely chopped

Preheat large heavy skillet or Dutch oven. Brown beef, bell peppers, onion, and spices together in canola oil. When beef is browned, add remaining ingredients and simmer 45 minutes, stirring occasionally. Garnish with dollop of sour cream, grated cheese, and finely chopped onion. Serves 8 to 10.

Leo's Tortilla Soup

Bean and Bacon Soup

- ¼ pound bacon
- ¼ cup chopped onion
- 1 quart water
- 1 can (about 10 ounces) bean with bacon soup
- 1½ cups cooked navy beans
  Roux (see page 12)
  Salt and pepper to taste

Sauté bacon; remove from pan and pour off fat. Measure 2 tablespoons bacon fat into large, heavy kettle. Cook onion in bacon fat until soft but not brown, 5 minutes. Add water, soup, and beans. Bring to a boil; thicken with a little roux, if desired. Add salt and pepper to taste. Add cooked bacon and serve. Makes 2½ quarts, or 10 one-cup servings.

Split Pea Soup

- 2 cups (1 pound) split peas
- 8 cups water
- 1 cup chopped onion
- 1 cup chopped ham, *or* meaty ham bone or hock
- 1 tablespoon salt
- ¼ teaspoon pepper
  Roux, if desired (see page 12)

Combine all ingredients in large soup kettle. Simmer for 1½ to 2 hours, or to desired consistency. Thicken slightly with a roux made of 2 tablespoons softened butter or margarine blended well with 2 tablespoons flour. Makes about 3 quarts, or 10 to 12 one-cup servings.

Leo's Tortilla Soup

- 2 tablespoons chicken base
- 4 cups diced canned tomatoes
- ¼ pound butter
- 1 cup canned diced green chilies
- 3 cups diced onions
- 10 cups water
- 5 cups dried refried beans
- 2 cups crushed heavy corn tortilla chips
- 1 tablespoon ground cumin
- 1 teaspoon garlic powder
- ⅔ cup diced green onion
- ⅔ cup fresh cilantro
  Tortilla chips
  Sour cream

In a large soup pot add chicken base, tomatoes, butter, green chilies, and onions. Cook until onions are translucent. Add water, dried beans, chips, and seasonings. Heat until thickened and beans are soft. Add green onions and cilantro about 5 minutes before serving. Garnish with crisp tortilla chips and sour cream. Yields 1 gallon, or 8 to 10 servings.

Sarah's Salad

Salads and Salad Dressings

Sarah's Salad

1	head iceberg lettuce
3	strips bacon
½	package (10 ounces) frozen peas
¼	teaspoon sugar
½	teaspoon salt
¼	teaspoon white pepper
½	cup Swiss cheese (2½ ounces), cut in strips
⅔	cup chopped green onion
¼	cup mayonnaise
¼	cup salad dressing (such as Miracle Whip®)

Wash and drain lettuce; dry thoroughly. Dice bacon and sauté until crisp; drain on paper towels. Run hot water over frozen peas and drain. Into salad bowl, tear lettuce into bite-sized pieces. Sprinkle with sugar, salt, and pepper. Add peas, Swiss cheese, green onion, mayonnaise, and salad dressing. Chill. Toss when ready to serve and garnish with bacon. Makes 8 servings.

Note: Ingredients may be layered, if desired, with mayonnaise spread on top as last layer. Cover tightly and refrigerate overnight.

Herbed Croutons for Salads

¼	cup grated Parmesan cheese
1	tablespoon oregano
1	tablespoon garlic powder
1	tablespoon basil
½	teaspoon salt
½	teaspoon freshly ground pepper
1	loaf dry bread, cubed (15 to 20 cups)
3	tablespoons oil

In small bowl, mix Parmesan cheese, oregano, garlic powder, basil, salt, and pepper; set aside. In large bowl, toss bread cubes with oil, then toss with cheese-herb mixture until well mixed. Spread on ungreased cookie sheet. Bake at 225 degrees for 1 hour or until crisp and lightly golden, stirring occasionally. Cool and store in plastic bags in cool place. Will keep about 1 month. Makes 15 to 20 cups.

Green Goddess Salad

1	head romaine lettuce
3	hard-cooked eggs, chopped
6	green onions, chopped
1	cup Green Goddess Dressing (below)
1	cup shrimp, fresh cooked or canned
1	cup croutons

Wash and drain lettuce; break into small pieces. Place on individual salad plates. Top with eggs and green onions. Drizzle dressing over salad, then place a few shrimp and croutons on each salad. Makes 6 salads.

Green Goddess Dressing

1	cup mayonnaise
½	cup thick sour cream
3	tablespoons tarragon vinegar
1	tablespoon lemon juice
⅓	cup finely chopped parsley
3	tablespoons finely chopped onion
3	tablespoons mashed anchovy fillets
1	tablespoon chopped chives
2	tablespoons chopped capers
1	small clove garlic, minced
¼	teaspoon pepper
½	teaspoon salt

Combine all ingredients in quart jar. Cover jar tightly and shake until mixture is well blended. Chill in refrigerator three to four hours. Shake well before using.

Green Salad

1	large head crisped lettuce
7	green onions, chopped, including tops
¼	head red cabbage
¼	large head white cabbage
3 to 4	medium tomatoes, cut in wedges
	Dressing (below)

Dressing

2	tablespoons mayonnaise
1	tablespoon chopped parsley
	Dash garlic salt
	Juice of 1 lemon (3 tablespoons)
2	tablespoons vinegar
	Salt and pepper
1	teaspoon paprika
½	cup heavy cream

Combine dressing ingredients and let stand for at least 30 minutes. Pour dressing over greens. Do not mix, but toss lightly just before serving. Garnish with tomato wedges. Makes about 12 servings. Dressing should be stored in refrigerator.

Mandarin Salad

2	quarts salad greens (any favorite variety), torn into pieces
2 to 3	ribs celery, cut diagonally
1	can (8 ounces) mandarin oranges, drained
2 to 3	green onions, chopped diagonally, including tops
1	cup grapes, any variety (seeded grapes should be halved and seeds removed)
½	cup pecans, coarsely chopped
	Dressing (below)

Clean and dry greens thoroughly. Toss all ingredients together. Just before serving, toss with dressing, using just enough to moisten lightly.

Dressing

2	tablespoons sesame seeds, toasted
3	tablespoons sugar or honey
1	teaspoon salt
	Dash pepper
¼	cup salad oil
2	tablespoons vinegar

Mix all ingredients together thoroughly. Dressing should be stored in refrigerator. Shake well before using.

Note: To toast sesame seeds, measure seeds into pie pan or baking sheet and place in 350-degree oven for about 10 minutes, stirring occasionally, until golden but not brown.

Salata (Greek Tossed Salad)

1	clove garlic, cut in half
½	head lettuce, torn
½	bunch endive, torn
3	tomatoes, cut in eighths (peeled if desired)
1	cucumber, peeled and sliced
6	green onions, thinly sliced
2	stalks celery, sliced
1	green pepper, slivered
2	tablespoons chopped fresh parsley
1	teaspoon oregano (optional)
1	teaspoon salt
⅛	teaspoon pepper
	Olive oil
	Wine vinegar
1	cooked beet, cut into shoestring strips
8	slices cheese, cut into shoestring strips (optional)
8	ripe Greek olives
¼	cup chickpeas (garbanzo beans), cooked
2	hard-cooked eggs, quartered

Rub a wooden salad bowl with garlic halves. Discard garlic. Combine next eleven ingredients. Toss with enough oil to coat. Add ¼ as much vinegar as oil and toss lightly. Garnish as desired with remaining ingredients. Makes 6 to 8 servings.

Spinach Salad

Spinach Salad

1	pound fresh spinach
½	cup salad oil
1	clove garlic, slivered
¼	cup vinegar
¼	cup lemon juice
½	teaspoon salt
	Dash pepper
2	tablespoons Parmesan cheese
2	hard-cooked eggs, sliced
6	slices crisp-cooked bacon, crumbled

Wash spinach; dry thoroughly and discard stems. Tear in pieces into salad bowl. Chill. Combine salad oil and garlic; refrigerate one hour. Discard garlic. Heat oil with vinegar, lemon juice, salt, pepper, and Parmesan cheese. Toss spinach with dressing. Garnish with eggs and bacon. Makes 4 to 5 servings.

Four-Bean Salad

½   cup sugar
½   teaspoon salt
⅔   cup oil
⅔   cup vinegar
1   can (16 ounces) garbanzo beans, drained
1   can (16 ounces) green beans, drained
1   can (16 ounces) yellow wax beans, drained
1   can (16 ounces) red kidney beans, drained
1   small onion, cut into rings
    Lettuce leaves

Combine sugar, salt, oil, and vinegar. Stir or shake until sugar is dissolved. Drain beans thoroughly and add onion rings. Pour dressing over beans and let marinate for 2 hours. Serve about 1 cup of mixture on each of 8 lettuce leaves. Makes 8 servings.

Golden Carrot Salad

3   medium carrots, peeled and sliced
1   teaspoon French dressing
⅓   cup celery, thinly sliced
1   tablespoon small sweet pickles, sliced
1   tablespoon mayonnaise or salad dressing

Slice carrots thin and cook in boiling salted water until tender-crisp. Drain. Drizzle French dressing over carrots. Chill 1 hour. Just before serving, add remaining ingredients. Mix lightly. Makes 6 servings.

Copper Penny Salad

1   can (10½ ounces) tomato soup
1   cup sugar
½   cup vinegar
½   cup salad oil
1   teaspoon salt
1   teaspoon dry mustard
4   pounds carrots, sliced and cooked
1   large onion, cut into thin rings
1   large green pepper, diced

Combine tomato soup, sugar, vinegar, salad oil, salt, and mustard in saucepan and bring to a boil. Pour hot dressing over carrots, onion, and green pepper. Marinate 24 hours. Serve hot or cold. Salad will keep up to two weeks in refrigerator. Makes 12 to 16 servings.

Carrot-Pineapple-Coconut Salad

5 or 6   medium carrots, finely shredded
1   small can (8 ounces) crushed pineapple
1   cup shredded or flaked coconut
¼   cup raisins
    Pinch salt

Mix all ingredients. Salad may be served with a dressing, if desired. Makes 4 to 6 servings.

Blueberry Salad

1   large package (6 ounces) raspberry gelatin
2   cups boiling water
1   package (8 ounces) cream cheese
1   can (15 ounces) blueberries, with syrup
1   can (15 ounces) crushed pineapple, drained
1   pint whipping cream
    Red leaf lettuce
    Fresh blueberries

Dissolve raspberry gelatin in 2 cups boiling water. Dissolve cream cheese in hot gelatin. Add blueberries and crushed pineapple. Whip cream and fold into gelatin mixture, reserving some for garnish. Spread mixture into 9x13-inch pan and refrigerate until set. Cut into squares.

When ready to serve, wash lettuce and dry thoroughly. Wash blueberries and set aside. Place lettuce leaf on salad plate, then square of blueberry salad. Garnish with fresh blueberries and dollop of whipped cream. Makes 10 to 12 servings.

Frozen Fruit Salad

- 1   small package (3 ounces) lemon gelatin
      Dash salt
- 1   cup boiling water
- 1   can (about 8 ounces) pineapple tidbits, *or* crushed pineapple, drained (reserve juice)
- ¼   cup lemon juice
- ⅓   cup mayonnaise
- 1   package (8 ounces) cream cheese, softened
- 1   banana, sliced
- ¼   cup maraschino cherries, halved
- ½   cup cut seedless grapes, mandarin oranges, or miniature marshmallows
- ¼   cup chopped nuts (optional)
- ½   cup heavy cream, whipped

Dissolve gelatin and salt in boiling water. Add water to pineapple juice to make ½ cup; stir into gelatin. Add lemon juice. Chill until thick but not set. Blend mayonnaise and cream cheese until smooth. Fold into chilled gelatin along with fruits, nuts, and whipped cream. Pour into two freezer trays or a 9x5-inch loaf pan. Freeze until firm, at least 3 to 4 hours. To serve, cut in squares or slices. Makes about 4 cups or 8 slices.

Note: Two cups whipped cream (1 cup before whipping), or 2 cups sour cream, may replace cream cheese. Other fruits (drained diced orange sections, drained canned fruit cocktail, etc.), totaling about 2 cups, may be used.

Fruit Salad

- 1   package (3 ounces) cooked lemon pudding and pie filling
- 1   can (about 16 ounces) fruit cocktail, drained (reserve juice)
- 1   can (13¼ ounces) pineapple tidbits, drained (reserve juice)
      Miniature marshmallows, as desired
- 1   cup heavy cream, whipped
- 2   bananas

Cook pudding as directed on package, using reserved fruit juices instead of water. Cool. Add drained fruit, marshmallows, and whipped cream. Slice bananas and add just before serving. May also be served as dessert. Makes 6 to 8 servings.

Note: Drained mandarin oranges and fresh strawberries may be used in place of or in addition to pineapple and fruit cocktail.

Apple Salad

- 8   tart apples, peeled, if desired, and chopped
- ½   cup diced celery
- ½   cup chopped dates
- ½   cup chopped nuts
- 2   tablespoons lemon juice
- 2   tablespoons sugar
      Maraschino cherries, if desired
      Salad dressing or whipped cream (optional)

Combine apples, celery, dates, nuts, and lemon juice. Sprinkle with sugar; toss and chill. Serve on lettuce leaf, garnished with cherries and dollop of salad dressing or whipped cream, if desired. Makes 10 to 12 servings.

Cranberry Salad

- 1   cup water
- 2   cups sugar
- 4   cups cranberries
- 2   cups miniature marshmallows, *or* cut large marshmallows
- 2   apples, diced
- 3   bananas, sliced
- 3   cups orange sections
- ½   cup pecans

Combine water and sugar; boil until thickened to a syrup. Add cranberries; cook until cranberries burst. Remove from heat; let stand 10 minutes. Chill. Add remaining ingredients to cranberries and chill thoroughly. Serve on lettuce leaf. Top with whipped cream dressing, if desired. Makes 14 servings.

Cranberry Fluff Salad

2	cups raw cranberries, ground
1/2	cup sugar
3	apples, pared or unpared, as desired
1/2	cup chopped walnuts
3	cups miniature marshmallows
1/4	teaspoon salt
1	cup heavy cream, whipped

Combine cranberries and sugar; cover and chill overnight. Add apples, walnuts, marshmallows, and salt. Fold in whipped cream. Chill. Serve as a salad or dessert. Makes about 12 servings.

Orange Cloud Salad

1	large package (6 ounces) orange gelatin
16	ounces cottage cheese
12	ounces Cool Whip®
1	can (15½ ounces) crushed pineapple, drained
2	cans (11 ounces) mandarin oranges, drained

Sprinkle gelatin over cottage cheese; stir until dissolved. Add Cool Whip, pineapple, and mandarin oranges; mix well. Serve chilled.

Orange Cloud Salad

Cottage Cheese Fruit Salad

1   pint cottage cheese
2   cups (1-pound can) fruit cocktail with juioo
1   cup mandarin oranges, drained
1   cup pineapple chunks, drained
1   cup miniature marshmallows, *or* cut large marshmallows
½   cup flaked coconut
     Red grapes, halved

Mix all ingredients except grapes. Place in 8x4-inch loaf pan, and chill for several hours or overnight. Slice and serve on lettuce leaf. Garnish with red grapes. Makes 7 one-cup servings. Salad recipe may be doubled for 15 servings.

Princess Salad

1   can (16 ounces) pears, drained and cut up
2   cups miniature marshmallows
2   cups crushed pineapple, drained
¼   cup maraschino cherries, chopped
1   cup cream, whipped
     Lettuce
½   cup chopped nuts

Combine pears, marshmallows, pineapple, cherries, and unsweetened whipped cream. Place on lettuce bed and sprinkle with nuts. Makes 8 servings.

Cranberry Set Salad

1   large package (6 ounces) cherry-flavored gelatin
2   cups hot water
2   cups chipped ice, *or* 4 to 6 large ice cubes
1   can (16 ounces) jellied cranberry sauce
¼   teaspoon salt
½   cup sugar
1   large apple, diced
½   cup walnuts, chopped
1   small can crushed pineapple (do not drain)

Combine gelatin and hot water; stir until gelatin is completely dissolved. Cool with ice. Chill. When partially set, add cranberry sauce, salt, and sugar. Whip cranberry mixture until smooth; add apple, walnuts, and crushed pineapple. Chill until set. Serve on lettuce leaf, topped with whipped cream, if desired. Makes 10 to 12 servings.

Pear and Lime Salad

1   can (16 ounces) pear halves
1   small package (3 ounces) lime gelatin
1   cup boiling water
1   tablespoon lemon juice
1   package (3 ounces) cream cheese
1 to 2   tablespoons finely chopped nuts

Drain pears, reserving syrup. Add water to syrup to make 1 cup. Place pears, cut side up, in 8x8-inch square pan. Dissolve gelatin in boiling water. Add measured syrup and water and lemon juice; pour over pears. Chill until firm, about 3 hours. Divide cream cheese into 6 pieces; roll each piece into a ball, then roll in nuts. Cut gelatin into 6 servings; garnish with cheese balls. Serve on lettuce leaves. Makes 6 servings.

Raspberry Gelatin Salad

1¼   cups boiling water
1   small package (3 ounces) raspberry gelatin
1   package (10 ounces) frozen raspberries (do not thaw)
1   cup crushed pineapple, with juice
1   large banana, sliced
½   cup pecans
1   cup sour cream

Pour boiling water over gelatin. Stir for 2 minutes to dissolve thoroughly. Add raspberries, pineapple, banana, and pecans. Pour into individual molds and chill until firm; unmold onto lettuce leaves and garnish with sour cream. Makes 8 to 10 servings.

Pear Blush Salad

1   package (3 ounces) cream cheese, softened
¼   cup nuts, finely chopped
2   tablespoons maraschino cherries, chopped (include cherry juice)
1   large can (1 pound 14 ounces) pear halves, drained (reserve juice)
    Red food coloring
    Mint leaves

Combine cream cheese, nuts, cherries, and enough juice from pears to soften cheese. Put rounded teaspoon of cream cheese mixture in hollow of each of half the pears. Put 3 or 4 drops of red food coloring into reserved pear juice. Soak rest of pear halves in this liquid to tint pear pink, 5 to 10 minutes. Cover first halves with tinted halves. Stand pear on bed of lettuce and garnish with mint leaves. Makes 4 servings.

Six-Cup Salad

1   cup miniature marshmallows
1   cup pineapple chunks or tidbits, drained
1   cup mandarin oranges, drained
1   cup sour cream
1   cup coconut
1   cup maraschino cherry halves

In 2-quart container, carefully mix all ingredients together; chill 12 to 24 hours. Spoon onto lettuce leaves. Makes 6 to 8 servings.

Angel Salad

1   cup miniature marshmallows
3   bananas, chopped
1   cup pineapple chunks, drained and chopped
½   cup peanuts, crushed
2   tablespoons cornstarch
2   tablespoons sugar
1   cup pineapple juice
1   egg, beaten lightly
½   cup cream, whipped

Mix marshmallows and fruit; add peanuts. Make a cooked dressing of cornstarch, sugar, juice, and egg, blended together in that order. Heat, stirring constantly, until thickened. Cool and fold in whipped cream. Combine with salad mixture, just to moisten. Serve on greens. Makes 4 to 6 servings.

Crab and Avocado Salad

3   large avocados, peeled, pitted, cut into cubes
2   cans (7 ounces each) crab meat, rinsed and drained well, with pieces of cartilage removed
1   cup finely diced celery
½   cup finely sliced radishes
2   tablespoons lemon juice
2   tablespoons vinegar
4   tablespoons salad oil
2   tablespoons finely chopped green onions, including tops
    Dash cayenne pepper
    Salt to taste
3 or 4   tomatoes (optional)
    Louis Dressing (below)

Combine all ingredients except tomatoes. For each serving, spoon salad onto bed of lettuce on serving plate. Surround with tomato wedges, peeled if desired. Serve with Louis dressing. Makes 6 servings.

Louis Dressing

1   cup mayonnaise
⅓   cup chili sauce
2   tablespoons chopped parsley
1   tablespoon finely chopped green onion
    Dash cayenne pepper
¼   cup heavy cream, whipped

Combine first 5 ingredients; fold in whipped cream. Top each salad with 3 to 4 tablespoons dressing. Dressing should be stored in refrigerator.

Pear Blush Salad

Cantaloupe Salad

Cantaloupe Salad

- 2 small cantaloupes
- 6 peaches, peeled and sliced
- 2 cups honeydew melon, cubed
- 3 cups seeded grapes, halved
  French Fruit dressing (below)

Cut each cantaloupe lengthwise into 8 wedges; peel and chill. Coat peaches, honeydew melon, and grapes with dressing. (Keep remaining dressing for another use.) Chill 1 hour. For each serving, arrange 2 cantaloupe wedges to form oval or circle and fill centers with fruit mixture. Makes 8 servings.

French Fruit Dressing

- ⅓ cup sugar
- 1 teaspoon salt
- 1 teaspoon paprika
- ¼ cup orange juice
- 1 tablespoon lemon juice
- 1 tablespoon vinegar
- 1 cup salad oil
- 1 teaspoon onion, grated

Combine all ingredients in bottle or jar and cover. Shake thoroughly. Store any leftover dressing in refrigerator for later use. Shake well before each use.

Shrimp Salad

- 3 cans (5 ounces each) shrimp, *or* 1 pound fresh bay shrimp
- 1 cup chopped celery
- ¼ cup sliced green olives with pimiento
- 2 tablespoons lemon juice
- 3 hard-cooked eggs, cut in wedges
- 1 avocado, peeled and cut in wedges
- ¼ cup coarsely chopped cashews (optional)
  Dressing (below)

Combine shrimp, celery, olives, and lemon juice. Blend dressing ingredients thoroughly. When ready to serve, toss dressing with salad. Garnish with hard-cooked eggs, avocado, and cashews. Makes 6 to 8 servings.

Dressing

- 1 cup mayonnaise
- ⅓ cup chili sauce
- 1 teaspoon grated onion

Mix ingredients together. Toss with shrimp salad. Dressing should be stored in refrigerator.

Chicken Curry Salad with Fruit

- ⅔ cup mayonnaise
- 2 tablespoons lemon juice
- 1 teaspoon salt
- 1 teaspoon curry powder
- 2½ cups cooked chicken, diced
- 1 cup diced celery
  Salad greens
- ¼ cup slivered blanched almonds
- 1 avocado, sliced
- ½ cantaloupe, cut into wedges
- 1 cup seedless grapes
- 1 cup canned pineapple chunks, drained

Blend mayonnaise, lemon juice, salt, and curry powder. Combine chicken and celery; mix lightly. Pour mayonnaise mixture over chicken mixture. Chill. Just before serving, mound salad in center of serving platter lined with salad greens. Sprinkle with almonds. Garnish with avocado and fruits. Makes 6 servings.

Thousand Island Dressing

- 1½ cups Miracle Whip®
- ¼ cup pickle relish
- ⅓ cup chili sauce
- ⅓ cup milk (enough for desired consistency)

Combine ingredients; mix well and chill. Stir before serving. Makes 2 cups. Dressing should be stored in refrigerator.

Buttermilk Dressing

1½	cups mayonnaise
¼	cup buttermilk (or more, to desired consistency)
½	teaspoon salt (or to taste)
	Pepper to taste
¼	teaspoon onion salt
¼	teaspoon garlic salt
2	tablespoons fresh chopped parsley

Combine all ingredients. Let stand half a day before using. Crumbled bleu cheese may be added. Makes about 2 cups. Dressing should be stored in refrigerator.

Boiled Salad Dressing

1	tablespoon salt
2	teaspoons dry mustard
6	tablespoons sugar
	Few grains cayenne pepper
1	teaspoon celery seed
1	tablespoon flour
4	egg yolks
3	tablespoons margarine, melted
1½	cups milk
½	cup vinegar

Combine all ingredients except vinegar. Cook over low heat until mixture thickens, stirring constantly. Add vinegar, blend well, and chill. Will keep about two months in refrigerator. Makes a very good coleslaw dressing. Makes about 1 quart.

Sour Cream Herb Dressing

1	cup sour cream
2	tablespoons vinegar
1	teaspoon sugar
½	teaspoon salt
½	teaspoon celery seed
	Dash pepper
¼	teaspoon crumbled dried thyme

Blend all ingredients together. Chill. Makes about 1 cup. Dressing should be stored in refrigerator.

Lion House French Dressing

1	cup sugar
1	cup catsup
1	cup vinegar
1	cup oil
1	teaspoon mustard
¼	teaspoon pepper
½	cup onion, chopped
1½	teaspoons lemon juice
½	teaspoon Worcestershire sauce

Combine ingredients and mix or shake well. Makes 1 quart. Dressing should be stored in refrigerator.

Bleu Cheese Dressing

2	cups mayonnaise
1	small onion, grated
4	tablespoons cider vinegar
	Dash garlic salt
1	cup sour cream
¾	cup chopped fresh parsley
3	ounces (or more) bleu cheese

Combine all ingredients except bleu cheese and mix well. Crumble in bleu cheese. Makes about 1 quart. Store dressing in refrigerator.

Poppy Seed Dressing

¾	cup sugar
1	tablespoon dry mustard
½	teaspoon salt
⅓	cup cider vinegar
1	tablespoon onion juice
1	cup salad oil
1½	tablespoons poppy seeds

In medium-sized bowl, combine sugar, mustard, salt, vinegar, and onion juice. Using portable mixer, beat in oil gradually, until mixture is thick and smooth. Stir in poppy seeds; store covered in refrigerator. Makes 1⅔ cups.

Strawberry Dressing for Fruit Salad

1   package (10 ounces) frozen strawberries, thawed and drained
⅔   cup mayonnaise
1   carton (8 ounces) strawberry-flavored yogurt

Combine strawberries and mayonnaise; fold in yogurt. Cover and chill 1 hour. Serve over fresh fruit, honeydew wedges, and strawberries. Garnish with mint. Makes 3 cups. Dressing should be stored in refrigerator.

Honey Lime Dressing for Fresh Fruit

1   pound honey
5   tablespoons limeade concentrate

Beat together with hand mixer for about 2 to 3 minutes. Store at room temperature. Serve over fresh fruit.

Famous Fruit Salad Dressing

⅓   cup sugar
1   teaspoon flour
1   egg yolk
½   cup canned pineapple juice or orange juice
2   tablespoons lemon juice
1   teaspoon celery seed (optional)
½   cup heavy cream, whipped

In small saucepan, combine sugar, flour, egg yolk, and pineapple juice; stir until smooth. Cook over low heat until thickened, stirring constantly. Add lemon juice and celery seed; chill. Fold in whipped cream just before serving. Store dressing in refrigerator.

Lamb Stew

2	pounds lean lamb meat, cut in chunks
2	tablespoons flour
1½	teaspoons salt
¼	teaspoon pepper
2	tablespoons cooking oil
1	garlic clove, minced or pressed
1	onion, finely chopped
½	cup celery, thinly sliced
½	teaspoon dill weed
2	cups water
1½	teaspoons sugar
1	cup carrots, sliced
1	cup green beans
1	cup small white onions

Dredge lamb chunks in flour, salt, and pepper. Brown slightly in hot oil in Dutch oven or large frying pan. Add garlic, onion, and celery to meat as it browns. Add dill weed and water; cover and simmer until meat is tender, about 2 hours. Add sugar and remaining vegetables, and simmer until vegetables are tender, 10 to 15 minutes. Thicken liquid with a little additional flour mixed with cold water, if desired. Makes 6 to 8 servings. Good served with dumplings.

Note: This recipe may also be made with leftover cooked roast lamb. Follow directions above, except cooked meat can simply be trimmed from the bone, cut in pieces, and warmed in leftover gravy, canned gravy, or gravy made from a mix. Cook and add vegetables and seasonings separately. Adjust seasonings to taste.

Rossini Tournedos

5	pounds tenderloin of beef, center cut
	Salt and pepper
	Melted butter

Cut raw beef into diagonal slices, about 1 inch thick, then cut each slice in half to make 2 small, thick steaks. Rub each slice with salt and pepper. Place in single layer in shallow roasting pan. Brush with melted butter. Bake at 450 degrees for about 10 minutes (or to desired doneness), without turning. Serve both halves of the slice on dinner plate, with generous spoonful of Bordelaise Sauce (below) on one half, Bearnaise Sauce (below) on the other. Makes 10 servings.

Bordelaise Sauce

2	tablespoons butter
1	thin slice onion
2	tablespoons flour
1	cup beef broth
¼	teaspoon salt
⅛	teaspoon pepper
1	tablespoon chopped parsley
1	bay leaf, crushed
¼	teaspoon thyme

Heat butter in frying pan until golden brown. Add onion and cook until tender. Blend in flour and cook until a deep brown color. Remove from heat and stir in broth; stir and boil for 1 minute. Add salt, pepper, parsley, bay leaf, and thyme. Serve with Rossini tournedos. Makes about 1 cup.

Note: For an excellent variation, add ¼ pound sliced mushrooms sautéed in 2 tablespoons butter.

Bearnaise Sauce

½	cup apple juice
2	tablespoons white vinegar
2	small green onions, chopped
1	tablespoon crushed dried tarragon
¼	teaspoon pepper
3	egg yolks, beaten
½	cup butter, melted
2	teaspoons lemon juice

¼ teaspoon salt
Dash cayenne pepper

In small, heavy saucepan, combine apple juice, vinegar, onions, tarragon, and pepper. Boil until mixture is reduced by half, or to about ½ cup. Add gradually to egg yolks, stirring well to blend. Return to heat and cook until thickened and creamy, stirring constantly. Beat in butter, lemon juice, salt, and cayenne pepper. Serve with Rossini tournedos. Makes 1 cup.

Chateaubriand (Roast Beef Tenderloin)

5 pounds tenderloin of beef, center cut
Garlic (optional)
Salt
Soft butter, *or* 3 strips bacon

Trim excess fat or connective tissue from meat. Place meat in shallow roasting pan; rub with cut garlic and salt. Brush with soft butter or top with half strips of bacon. Bake at 450 degrees for 45 to 60 minutes (until meat is red to pink inside). Slit meat with tip of paring knife to check doneness. (Or use a meat thermometer and cook to desired doneness.)

Remove meat to warm platter and slice diagonally in about ½-inch-thick slices. Serve two slices per person, with Bordelaise Sauce or Bearnaise Sauce (above). Also good served with mushrooms, sliced and sautéed in butter. Makes about 10 servings.

Roast Beef and Yorkshire Pudding

Standing rib roast of beef (5 to 7 pounds)
½ teaspoon salt
⅛ teaspoon pepper

Wipe beef well with damp cloth. Rub the lean portion with salt and pepper. Insert meat thermometer through outside fat into thickest part of muscle. Be careful that tip of thermometer does not touch bone. Place roast in shallow roasting pan and roast at 325 degrees until internal temperature reaches 140 degrees for rare (about 20 minutes per pound), 160 degrees for medium (about 25 minutes per pound), 170 degrees for well done (about 30 minutes per pound).

As soon as roast is done, remove from oven to warm platter and turn oven temperature to 425 degrees. Keep meat warm while making pudding and gravy (below). Let meat stand a while for easier slicing. Makes 8 servings.

Yorkshire Pudding

2 eggs
1 cup milk
1 cup sifted flour
½ teaspoon salt
2 tablespoons roast beef drippings

Beat eggs, milk, flour, and salt until batter is smooth and creamy. Pour drippings into 10-inch pie pan. Tilt pan till drippings cover bottom of pan. Pour in batter. Bake at 425 degrees about 25 minutes, or until pudding is puffed and nicely browned. Serve immediately with roast beef.

Make gravy from the rest of the drippings, using roux to thicken as desired, and diluting with water or beef broth, if necessary.

Beef Wellington

3½ to 4	pounds beef tenderloin
	Lion House Pie Dough (page 111)
8	ounces liver sausage or liver paté
1	egg, beaten slightly

Place meat on rack in shallow roasting pan and roast uncovered at 425 degrees for 20 to 30 minutes, till rare to medium. Remove from oven and let stand for 30 minutes.

In the meantime, make Lion House Pie Dough for 9-inch double-crust pie (page 111). Or purchase puff pastry for patty shells from grocery freezer case. Pinch individual shells together, then roll into 18x14-inch rectangle, ¼-inch thick. Spread paté on pastry, then place cooked tenderloin lengthwise, top side down, in center of pastry. Bring long sides of pastry up over bottom of tenderloin; brush with egg and seal the two sides together. Trim ends of pastry and fold over; brush with egg and seal.

Carefully transfer pastry-wrapped meat, seam side down, to baking sheet. Cut decorative shapes from pastry trimmings and arrange on top. Brush egg over all. Bake at 425 degrees for 30 minutes or until delicately browned. Let stand 10 minutes before carving. Makes 6 to 8 servings.

Party Swiss Steak

4	pounds beef round, top or bottom, cut about ½-inch thick
¾	cup flour
4 to 6	tablespoons shortening
1	tablespoon salt
¼	teaspoon pepper
½	teaspoon thyme
2	cups water
1	cup chopped celery
1	cup chopped green pepper
2	cans (1 pound each) tomatoes (about 4 cups)
½	pound mozzarella cheese, thinly sliced

Cut meat into serving-size pieces. Dredge with ½ cup flour. Brown in hot shortening. Remove meat to large Dutch oven or roasting pan. Blend remaining flour with hot drippings; add seasonings. Gradually blend in water. Add vegetables. Cook and stir until slightly thickened. Pour mixture over meat and bake at 325 degrees for 2½ to 3 hours, or until meat is tender. Top with slices of cheese. Return to oven just until cheese melts. Serve at once. Makes 8 to 10 servings.

Beef and Seven Vegetables

1	tablespoon cooking oil
3	cups sliced cooked roast beef (about 1½x2-inch strips), *or* 1½ pounds fresh lean beef, cut into strips
2½	cups carrots, cut in thin slices
1½	cups sliced green pepper
1½	cups sliced onion
2½	cups slant-cut celery
1	can (about 4 ounces) bamboo shoots, drained
4	cups beef stock, *or* 4 beef bouillon cubes and 4 cups water
½ to ¾	cup soy sauce
3	tablespoons cornstarch in ¼ cup cold water
15	cherry tomatoes
1	cup fresh or frozen snow peas, *or* broccoli florets
	Cooked rice or Chinese noodles

Heat oil in frying pan. Add beef and brown lightly; remove meat. Add carrots and green pepper to pan; stir-fry for 1 minute. Add onions and celery; stir-fry for 1 minute. Add bamboo shoots. Remove vegetables and keep warm. Vegetables should remain crisp.

In heavy pot, bring soup stock and soy sauce to a gentle boil; thicken with cornstarch-water mixture. Add tomatoes, snow peas or broccoli, stir-fried vegetables, and meat; heat gently. Serve over rice or Chinese noodles. Makes 8 servings.

Beef and Seven Vegetables

Sweet and Sour Beef

1 pound tender lean beef, cut into thin strips (beef is easier to cut if partially frozen)
1 tablespoon cooking oil
 Sweet and Sour Sauce (below)
1 green pepper, cut into ¼-inch strips
1 can (about 15 ounces) chunk pineapple, drained (reserve juice for sauce)
 Hot cooked rice

Lightly brown in oil half of meat strips at a time. Add sweet and sour sauce and green pepper to meat strips; heat together until green pepper wilts but does not lose its color. Add pineapple chunks. Reheat and serve over cooked rice. Makes 5 servings.

Sweet and Sour Sauce

2 tablespoons cornstarch
6 tablespoons sugar
 Pineapple juice from above with water added to make 1½ cups
3 tablespoons vinegar
2 tablespoons soy sauce (or to taste)

Mix cornstarch with sugar. Add pineapple-water mixture, vinegar, and soy sauce. Boil together until thickened.

Stir-Fried Beef and Peppers

1 pound lean beef, cut in paper-thin strips (beef is easier to cut if partially frozen)
3 tablespoons soy sauce
1 tablespoon lemon juice
4 teaspoons cornstarch
¼ teaspoon sugar
⅛ teaspoon ground ginger
½ cup salad oil
½ pound mushrooms, thickly sliced
2 medium onions, quartered
2 small green peppers, cut in squares or strips
½ teaspoon salt

Combine meat strips with soy sauce, lemon juice, cornstarch, sugar, and ginger. Let stand while preparing vegetables.

Heat salad oil in large frying pan or Dutch oven. Stir-fry mushrooms, onions, green peppers, and salt until vegetables are tender-crisp, about 5 minutes. Remove vegetables from pan and reserve oil.

Stir-fry meat mixture in the hot oil a minute or two, until it loses its pink color. Add vegetables and stir until hot. Serve with cooked rice. Makes 4 to 6 servings.

Lion House Meat Loaf

2 pounds lean ground beef
1 teaspoon salt
3 eggs, beaten slightly
¾ cup dry bread crumbs
 Meat Loaf Sauce (below)

Mix ground beef, salt, eggs, bread crumbs, and half the sauce until well blended. Mold into one large or two small loaf pans. Bake at 350 degrees for 1½ hours for large loaf, about 1 hour for smaller ones. Remove from oven and allow to stand for about 10 minutes for easier slicing. Serve with remaining sauce. Makes 8 to 10 servings.

Meat Loaf Sauce

½ cup chopped onion
2 tablespoons shortening
1 can (10½ ounces) tomato soup
1 teaspoon Worcestershire sauce
 Few grains pepper
¼ cup water

Sauté onion in shortening until tender. Add soup, Worcestershire sauce, pepper, and water. Simmer a few minutes to blend flavors.

Beef Parmesan

6 cubed steaks
¼ cup evaporated milk
 Dry bread crumbs
2 tablespoons cooking oil
 Salt
½ cup Parmesan cheese
6 slices mozzarella cheese
1 can (15 ounces, or about 2 cups) tomato sauce

1½ cups tomato juice
¼ cup water
½ teaspoon garlic powder
2 tablespoons chopped onion
   Dash thyme
   Dash pepper

Dip steaks in evaporated milk, then in bread crumbs; brown in hot oil. Remove from frying pan and place in 9x13-inch baking pan. Sprinkle with salt and half the Parmesan cheese. Place one slice mozzarella cheese on top of each steak. In small saucepan, combine remaining ingredients except Parmesan cheese. Heat, then pour over meat and cheese. Sprinkle with remaining Parmesan cheese. Bake at 350 degrees for 30 minutes. Makes 6 servings.

Savory Steak Italia

1½ pounds round steak, cut into 6 serving portions, ¾-inch thick
3 tablespoons flour
1 teaspoon salt
¼ teaspoon oregano
¼ teaspoon pepper (or to taste)
1 can (15½ ounces) spaghetti sauce with mushrooms
1 package (9 ounces) frozen Italian green beans
1 can (6 ounces) whole onions, drained

Rub steak with ⅓ of a mixture of flour, salt, oregano, and pepper; reserve remainder of mixture for sauce. In large skillet over medium heat, brown both sides of steak in small amount of hot cooking oil. Remove browned pieces to shallow baking dish (about 11x7 inches).

Heat sauce and remaining flour mixture to boiling, stirring constantly. Pour over steak; cover, and bake at 375 degrees for 45 minutes. Add vegetables; cover and bake another 45 minutes or until meat is tender. Makes 6 servings.

Beef Goulash

2 pounds beef chuck, cut into cubes about 1½ inches square
2 tablespoons oil
2 large onions, chopped
½ cup canned tomato soup
2 bouillon cubes, *or* 2 teaspoons soup base
1½ cups water
1 tablespoon paprika
1 teaspoon vinegar
   Cooked noodles

Brown meat in oil in skillet; remove from pan. Cook onions in same skillet until golden brown. Add meat, tomato soup, bouillon cubes, water, paprika, and vinegar; stir to mix. Lower heat and simmer about 2 hours or until meat is very tender. Serve with noodles. May also be cooked in a slow cooker, 6 to 8 hours on low heat. Makes 4 to 6 hearty servings.

Ground Beef Stroganoff

½ cup chopped onion
1 small clove garlic, minced
1 tablespoon butter or margarine
1 pound ground beef
2 tablespoons flour
1 teaspoon salt
¼ teaspoon pepper
¼ teaspoon paprika
1 cup sliced mushrooms
1 can (10½ ounces) cream of mushroom soup
1 cup sour cream
   Cooked rice or noodles

Sauté onion and garlic in a little butter or margarine in hot skillet. Stir in meat, flour, and seasonings; sauté about 5 minutes or until meat loses its color. Add mushrooms, then soup; simmer about 10 minutes. Stir in sour cream and heat, but do not boil. Add a little milk if needed. Season to taste. Serve on hot rice or noodles. Makes 4 to 6 servings.

Beef Stroganoff

1	clove garlic, cut in quarters
3	tablespoons olive oil or salad oil
1½	pounds lean round or sirloin steak, cut into thin bite-sized strips (1 inch long x ¼-inch thick)
¼ to ⅓	cup chopped onion
¾ to 1	teaspoon salt
⅛	teaspoon pepper
½	pound fresh mushrooms, washed and sliced
¼	cup flour
1½ to 2	cups milk
½ to 1	teaspoon paprika
1	cup sour cream
	Hot cooked rice or cooked noodles

In heavy skillet, heat garlic in oil for a few minutes, then remove and discard garlic. Add meat to skillet; brown slightly. Add onion, salt, and pepper. Cover and cook slowly for 35 to 45 minutes or until meat is completely tender, turning occasionally. Add more oil or water during cooking, if necessary. Add mushrooms. Cover and cook gently until mushrooms are tender, about 10 minutes.

With slotted spoon, remove meat and mushrooms to top of double boiler. Blend flour into drippings in pan. Slowly stir in milk. Cook and stir over medium heat until mixture thickens. Sprinkle in paprika until sauce is a light pink color. Add sauce to meat and mushroom mixture in double boiler. Add sour cream. Mix and heat well before serving, but do not boil. Adjust seasonings to taste. Serve over rice. Makes about 5 cups, or 4 to 5 servings.

Roulade of Beef

2	zucchini
2	onions
2	yellow squash
2	red bell peppers
2	green bell peppers
2	carrots
2	eye of round roasts (5 pounds each)
	Salt and pepper to taste
4	feet butcher's twine
¼	cup vegetable oil

Slice all vegetables lengthwise into ¼-inch strips (about the size and shape of a French fry). Reserve vegetables in refrigerator.

To prepare beef, first trim fat from roasts. Make a ¼-inch-deep cut down the length of each roast, running with the grain. Turn each roast so that the cut is ¼ inch above the cutting surface and begin to peel away the outside layer while rolling the beef away from the cut. Continue cutting and unrolling until you are left with a large sheet of meat. Place a layer of plastic wrap over the meat and use a mallet to tenderize and flatten it. (Tenderizing will help to expand the sheet of beef and smooth out any uneven spots left from cutting.) Season the beef with salt and pepper.

Arrange half the sliced vegetables in a pattern of colors on each sheet of beef so that they lie with the grain. Beginning at one edge, roll the beef so that the vegetables lie lengthwise in each roll. Placing the seam down, begin tying the beef with butcher's twine. Gently slide the string under each roll. Wrap the string around each roll and tie it tightly, placing one tie every 1½ to 2 inches.

Heat ¼ cup oil in large skillet or roasting pan. Brown beef rolls on all sides. Roast at 300 degrees until rolls reach an internal temperature of 145 degrees. Remove rolls from pan and allow to rest for 10 to 15 minutes.

In cooking pan, make sauce by bringing drippings to a boil and thickening with a mixture of cornstarch and water. Season to taste with salt and pepper. Slice the roulade across the grain to reveal the colorful spiral of vegetables. Top with the pan sauce and serve immediately. Makes 24 eight-ounce servings.

Beef Enchiladas

Sauce

3	cans (8 ounces each) tomato sauce
1	can (1 pound) chili con carne without beans
1	can (1 pound) kidney beans, ground
3	cups tomato juice

1 teaspoon basil
1 teaspoon chili powder
1 teaspoon oregano
½ teaspoon crushed red pepper

Mix all ingredients together in saucepan. Simmer on low heat for 30 minutes.

Filling

1 pound lean ground beef
½ cup tomato sauce
1 tablespoon taco seasoning
1 teaspoon crushed red pepper
2 teaspoons oregano
   Dash Tabasco® sauce

12 corn tortillas
1 cup grated Cheddar cheese
¼ cup ground onion

Brown ground beef in skillet. Add tomato sauce, taco seasoning, red pepper, oregano, and Tabasco sauce. Mix thoroughly. Divide beef mixture evenly onto corn tortillas. Sprinkle cheese and ground onion over beef mixture; roll up tortillas. Place seam side down in baking dish. Pour sauce over top. Bake at 350 degrees for 30 minutes. Sprinkle with additional cheese just before serving. Makes 12 enchiladas.

Beef Enchiladas

Stuffed Ground Beef

2	pounds lean ground beef
2	eggs, well beaten
1	cup dry bread crumbs
½	cup milk
2	teaspoons salt
¼	teaspoon pepper
2	cups herb stuffing mix
2	cans (10½ ounces each) cream of chicken soup
½	soup can water

Mix ground beef, eggs, bread crumbs, milk, salt, and pepper until well blended. Divide into 16 portions; flatten into thin patties. Make stuffing mix following package directions. Scoop about ¼ cup stuffing on each of 8 patties. Place a second patty on top, then press around edges to seal well. Place stuffed patties in shallow baking pan. Brown in 400-degree oven for about 25 minutes. Mix soup with water and pour over patties. Turn oven down to 350 degrees and continue baking for 30 minutes longer. To serve, spoon sauce remaining in baking pan over patties. Makes 8 servings.

Zucchini with Ground Beef

8	medium zucchini
1	pound lean ground beef
1	medium onion
1	clove garlic
2	tablespoons chopped green pepper
1	tablespoon salad oil
	Pinch salt, rosemary, thyme, marjoram, pepper
½	cup Parmesan cheese
⅔	cup cracker crumbs
1	can (8 ounces) tomato sauce
⅓	cup water
1	bouillon cube

Wash zucchini; boil in salted water 10 minutes. Cut lengthwise in halves and scoop out insides. Drain scooped-out portion and mash well. Sauté beef, onion, garlic, and green pepper in oil for 5 minutes. Stir with fork; add zucchini pulp, salt, herbs, all but 2 tablespoons cheese, and all but 2 tablespoons crumbs. Heap mixture into zucchini shells. Place in shallow baking dish. Heat tomato sauce, water, and bouillon cube until cube is dissolved. Pour over zucchini. Sprinkle with remaining cheese and crumbs. Bake 45 minutes at 350 degrees, basting once or twice. Makes 8 servings, 2 stuffed shells each.

Shepherd's Pie

1	can (about 10 ounces) gravy, *or* about 1½ cups leftover gravy
1	cup leftover roast lamb or beef
¾	cup sliced carrots, parboiled
½	cup chopped onions, parboiled
½	cup chopped celery, parboiled
½	cup frozen peas
	Salt and pepper to taste
3	potatoes, boiled, drained and mashed; *or* 3 cups mashed potatoes from dehydrated potato flakes or granules
½	cup grated cheese

Combine gravy, meat, carrots, onions, celery, and peas. Adjust seasonings to taste. Place mixture in 8x8-inch baking pan. "Frost" top with mashed potatoes; sprinkle with cheese. Bake at 350 degrees until cheese melts and mixture bubbles. Makes 6 servings.

Note: You may use raw meat, one-half pound of either beef or lamb cubes. Brown well in a little cooking oil, then add water to cover; add carrots, onions, and celery after meat has simmered about 1 hour. Cook until meat and vegetables are tender. Thicken with about 2 tablespoons flour shaken with ½ cup cold water in ½-pint jar. Proceed as above.

Beef Pastries

	Pastry for 9-inch two-crust pie
1	pound lean ground beef
1	small can mushrooms, undrained
½	cup chopped onions
½	cup chopped celery
3	tablespoons sweet pickle relish
1	can (10½ ounces) cream of mushroom soup

1   can (about 10 ounces) beef gravy, *or*
     about 1½ cups leftover gravy

Roll out half of pastry dough and cut out 6 five-inch circles. Combine ground beef, mushrooms, onions, and celery. Cook in frying pan until meat loses its color; drain. Add pickle relish and soup. Place a large scoop of meat mixture in center of each pastry circle.

Roll out remaining pastry and cut out another 6 circles. Roll each of these circles a little larger than the first 6. Place over meat filling, moisten, and seal edges. Bake at 500 degrees for 10 minutes or until golden brown. Serve topped with beef gravy. Makes 6 servings.

Macaroni and Beef Bake

2   tablespoons cooking oil
2   pounds ground beef (use fresh meat or
     leftover roast beef, ground)
⅔   cup finely chopped onion
⅓   pound (1 cup) macaroni
4   cups tomato juice
1   can (10½ ounces) tomato soup
1½   cups shredded Cheddar cheese
1½   teaspoons chili powder
     Few grains salt and pepper

In frying pan in hot oil brown ground beef, onion, and macaroni. Add tomato juice, tomato soup, half the cheese, chili powder, salt, and pepper. Bake in large casserole at 350 degrees for about 1 hour, or until macaroni is tender. Cover with cheese and return to oven until cheese melts. Makes 8 servings.

Porcupine Meatballs

1   pound lean ground beef
⅓   cup uncooked rice
¼   cup chopped onion
¼   cup water
1   teaspoon salt
     Dash pepper
1   can (10½ ounces) condensed tomato
     soup

½   teaspoon chili powder
½   cup water

Combine beef, rice, onion, water, salt, and pepper. Shape into about 15 one-inch balls. Blend soup and chili powder; stir in ½ cup water. Bring to a boil, and add meatballs. Cover and simmer gently one hour, stirring occasionally. Makes about 6 servings.

Sweet and Sour Meatballs

2½   pounds ground pork
5   pounds ground beef
2¼   teaspoons pepper
2¼   teaspoons garlic powder
3   cups bread crumbs
1   cup milk
2½   cups chopped onions
8   eggs
⅓   cup flour
1½   cups tomato sauce
4½   teaspoons salt
2¼   teaspoons soy sauce
     Sweet and Sour Sauce (below)

Mix all ingredients together. Form into meatballs; place on baking pans or cookie sheets. Bake at 350 degrees for 20 minutes. Remove from pan and place in large cooking pot. Pour sweet and sour sauce over meatballs and simmer for approximately 1½ hours on low heat. Makes 15 to 20 servings.

Sweet and Sour Sauce

¼   teaspoon salt
2½   quarts pineapple juice plus 1½ cups water
2   quarts catsup
2   cups sugar
⅔   cups rice vinegar
3   tablespoons soy sauce
3   cans (15 ounces each) pineapple tidbits,
     drained

Mix all ingredients together, except pineapple tidbits; bring to boil. Add 3 cups water mixed with 2¼ cups cornstarch. Stir until thickened. Add pineapple. Pour over meatballs. Makes 1 gallon.

Ham with Pineapple Sauce

Ham with Maple Syrup and Cider Glaze

1 cup maple syrup
½ cup sweet cider
Ham
Whole cloves

Combine syrup and cider and set aside. Place ham in roasting pan, fat side up. Score fat with sharp knife, diagonally in two directions, forming diamond shapes. Stud points of diamonds with whole cloves. Brush entire surface with syrup and cider glaze. Bake at 325 degrees, basting occasionally with glaze. To develop a fully cooked ham's flavor and tenderness, bake 15 to 20 minutes per pound.

Ham with Orange Glaze

1 can (6 ounces) frozen orange juice
¼ cup firmly packed brown sugar
½ teaspoon dry mustard
1 teaspoon Worcestershire sauce
6- to 7- pound ham

Combine first 4 ingredients and heat, stirring constantly, until sugar dissolves. Makes about 1 cup.

Place ham in large, shallow baking pan. Bake at 350 degrees, 15 to 20 minutes per pound. After 30 minutes baking time, spread top generously with orange glaze. Continue baking 1 hour, basting every 10 minutes with more orange glaze, until meat is richly glazed.

Lion House Pineapple Sauce for Ham

3 cups pineapple juice
¾ cup brown sugar
3 tablespoons cornstarch

Combine ingredients; heat and stir in heavy saucepan until slightly thickened. Pour over ham and bake. Sauce may also be ladled over ham at serving time. Makes about 1 quart.

Mustard Sauce for Ham

½ cup brown sugar
1 tablespoon flour
¼ cup dry mustard
3 egg yolks, slightly beaten
½ cup vinegar
½ cup water
¼ cup margarine

Combine dry ingredients well. Add to egg yolks in small saucepan; mix well. Add vinegar and water. Cook over low heat until thickened, stirring constantly. Add margarine and remove from heat. Stir well and cool. Leftover sauce will keep in refrigerator several weeks. Makes 2 cups.

Buffet Ham

1 boneless ham (7 or 8 pounds)
Prepared mustard
1½ cups orange juice
1½ cups maple syrup
1 teaspoon allspice
½ teaspoon mace
½ teaspoon cinnamon
2 teaspoons paprika
3 cups cream (part whipping cream, part half-and-half)

Have butcher cut ham in half-inch slices. Spread one side of each ham slice generously with mustard. Arrange in large roasting pan, slices overlapping. In medium bowl, combine orange juice, syrup, allspice, mace, cinnamon, and paprika; pour over ham. Bake uncovered at 350 degrees for 30 minutes. Remove from oven and pour cream over ham. Return to oven and bake about 1 hour longer. Spoon hot sauce over each slice at serving time. Makes about 16 servings.

Party Ham Roll-Ups

        25   slices ham (about 5 pounds)
        25   slices Swiss cheese (about 1½ pounds)
             Cornbread Stuffing (below)
             Apricot Sauce (below)

Lay out ham and cheese slices. Spoon about ⅓ cup Cornbread Stuffing in center of each ham slice. Lay slice of Swiss cheese on top of stuffing. Roll up and secure with toothpick. Place in shallow baking dish. Bake at 350 degrees for 45 minutes. Spoon 2 or 3 tablespoons sauce over each roll-up at serving time. Makes 25 servings. (Recipe may be halved, if desired.)

Cornbread Stuffing

         1   pan (8x8-inch) cornbread, any favorite
             recipe or package mix
         1   cup finely chopped celery and leaves
         4   tablespoons finely chopped onion
         1   cup butter or margarine
         ½   cup apricot preserves
         ¼   cup water

Cook celery and onion in margarine until soft. Stir in preserves and water. Toss mixture lightly with crumbled cornbread. Add more water, if desired, for a moister stuffing.

Apricot Sauce

         1   tablespoon cornstarch
         2   tablespoons brown sugar
         1   cup water
         1   cup pineapple juice
         1   tablespoon butter
         ¼   cup apricot preserves

In small saucepan, mix cornstarch and brown sugar. Add water and pineapple juice; stir over medium heat until mixture boils and thickens. Stir in butter and preserves.

Ham-Cheese Strata

         8   slices firm white bread, crusts removed
         4   slices sharp Cheddar cheese
         1   cup chopped cooked ham
         4   eggs, beaten
         2   cups milk
         1   teaspoon finely chopped onion
             Dash pepper
         ½   teaspoon salt
         ¼   teaspoon dry mustard

Arrange 4 slices bread in bottom of 8x8-inch baking pan. Cover with slices of cheese, ham, and remaining bread. Combine eggs, milk, onion, and seasonings; pour over sandwiches. Let stand 1 hour. Bake at 325 degrees for 1 hour or until lightly browned and puffy. Let stand a few minutes; cut into squares. Makes 4 to 6 servings.

Ham and Green Noodle Casserole

         1   cup sour cream
         1   can (10½ ounces) Cheddar cheese soup
         2   cups (6 ounces) uncooked Green Noodles
             (below), cooked and drained
        1½   cups cooked, diced ham
         ½   cup pitted ripe olives, sliced
         1   can (2½ ounces) mushrooms, drained
         ¾   teaspoon prepared mustard
         ¼   cup milk
         ⅛   teaspoon pepper
         1   cup grated sharp Cheddar cheese

Combine sour cream and soup. Beat till smooth. Add remaining ingredients except cheese. Place in 8x8-inch baking pan or casserole. Sprinkle with grated cheese. Bake at 350 degrees for 25 minutes. Makes 8 servings.

Green Noodles

         1   package (10 ounces) frozen chopped
             spinach
         2   eggs
         ½   teaspoon salt
        2½   cups flour

Cook spinach according to package directions. Drain well, pressing out moisture with back of spoon. Force spinach through food mill or puree in blender. In mixing bowl beat eggs and salt; beat in spinach purée. Add enough flour to make a firm dough. Knead thoroughly. Cut dough into 4 pieces and let rest 30 minutes.

On floured board, roll each piece of dough into a very thin 12-inch square. As each square is rolled, remove it to a kitchen towel and let dry about 1 hour. Cut into strips about ¼-inch wide. Cook noodle strips in large quantity of boiling salted water 8 to 10 minutes. Drain and rinse thoroughly. Makes about 1 pound noodles.

Ham Loaf with Mustard Sauce

2	pounds ground pork
1	pound ground ham
1	egg, beaten
1½	cups milk
¼	teaspoon salt
1	cup dry bread crumbs or soda cracker crumbs
3	tablespoons tomato soup
½	teaspoon paprika
2	tablespoons chopped onion
2	tablespoons chopped green pepper
	Onion slices
	Mustard Sauce (below)

Have butcher grind pork and ham together. Mix all ingredients and place in buttered 9x5-inch loaf pan, placing onion slices on top. Bake at 350 degrees for 1½ hours. Serve with Mustard Sauce. Makes 8 to 10 servings.

Mustard Sauce

½	cup tomato soup
½	cup vinegar
¼	pound butter
½	cup prepared mustard
½	cup sugar
3	egg yolks

Combine all ingredients and cook slowly until thick, on low heat. Serve on ham loaf. Makes about 2½ cups.

Mint Sauce for Lamb

½	cup vinegar
1 to 2	tablespoons sugar
¼	cup chopped fresh mint leaves

Scald vinegar; add sugar and stir until dissolved. Add mint and allow sauce to brew for an hour or more before serving.

Barbecued Spareribs

3 to 4	pounds pork spareribs
1	tablespoon salt
½	teaspoon black pepper
2	onions, chopped
2	tablespoons vinegar
1	teaspoon chili powder
2	tablespoons Worcestershire sauce
¾	cup water
½	teaspoon cayenne pepper
¾	cup catsup
1	teaspoon paprika

Sprinkle spareribs with salt and pepper. Place in roasting pan and cover with onions. Combine remaining ingredients and pour over meat. Cover and bake at 350 degrees about 2 hours. Baste and turn ribs once or twice. Uncover last half-hour for browning. Makes 6 servings.

Stuffed Pork Chops

6	pork chops, 1 inch thick with pocket
½	cup finely chopped onion
½	cup finely chopped celery
¼	cup butter
1	cup chicken stock
1	teaspoon salt
1	teaspoon poultry seasoning
1	teaspoon sage
3	cups ground dry bread crumbs
½	teaspoon salt
½	teaspoon pepper
1	teaspoon paprika
1	can cream of celery soup
⅓	can water

Have butcher cut a pocket-slit in each pork chop. Sauté onion and celery in butter. Mix in stock and seasonings. Remove from heat and mix in bread crumbs until moistened. Stuff each pork chop with ½ cup stuffing. Coat each chop with mixture of fine bread crumbs, salt, pepper, and paprika. Place chops in shallow baking dish. Combine celery soup and water and pour over chops. Bake at 350 degrees for 1½ to 2 hours. Makes 6 servings.

Apple 'n' Orange Pork Chops

8 pork chops, about ½-inch thick
Salt and pepper
1 tablespoon shortening
½ cup chopped onion
1 cup uncooked long-cooking rice
1½ cups water
1 cup peeled and chopped tart apple
1 cup orange sections
1½ teaspoons salt
⅛ teaspoon pepper
⅛ teaspoon poultry seasoning (optional)

Trim excess fat from pork chops; season lightly with salt and pepper. Brown quickly in shortening, and remove from skillet. Pour from skillet all but 2 tablespoons of the drippings. Sauté onion in drippings. Add all remaining ingredients except pork chops; mix well. Pour into greased 2- or 3-quart shallow casserole (9x13-inch). Arrange chops on this mixture. Cover and bake at 350 degrees for about 45 minutes. Makes 8 servings.

Note: This recipe is also very good without apple or oranges or with no fruit.

Sweet and Sour Pork

2 pounds lean pork, about ½-inch thick
2 tablespoons cornstarch
¼ cup soy sauce
3 tablespoons oil
2 cups carrots, cut in diagonal chunks
3 small onions, cut in quarters
1 green pepper, cut in strips
1 can (20 ounces) chunk pineapple, drained
3 tablespoons cornstarch
3 tablespoons brown sugar
2 cups pineapple juice
¼ cup vinegar
⅓ cup soy sauce
Cooked rice

Cut pork into 2-inch strips. Mix 2 tablespoons cornstarch and ¼ cup soy sauce. Marinate pork in this mixture for 1 to 2 hours or overnight, in refrigerator. Drain, reserving marinade. Stir-fry meat in hot oil until evenly browned and tender, about 10 minutes. Remove meat from pan. Stir-fry carrots and onions in same pan, using more oil, if necessary. Cover and cook on low heat until tender-crisp, about 10 minutes. Add green pepper and pineapple. Return meat to pan, then stir in marinade.

In the meantime, make sweet and sour sauce: Mix cornstarch and sugar in small saucepan. Add pineapple juice, vinegar, and soy sauce. Cook and stir until thickened and clear. Pour over meat and vegetables; heat until flavors are blended, about 10 minutes. Adjust seasonings to taste. Serve over cooked rice. Makes 8 to 10 servings.

Pork Chow Mein

1 pound lean pork, cubed
Oil
1 cup chopped onion
1 cup slant-cut celery
½ cup canned sliced bamboo shoots
1 can (2½ ounces) mushrooms
1 cup bean sprouts
1 cup chicken stock
½ teaspoon sugar
2 tablespoons soy sauce
1½ tablespoons cornstarch
Chow mein noodles or hot cooked rice

Stir-fry cubed pork in oiled frying pan until browned and tender. Remove meat from pan. Add vegetables and more oil, if necessary, and stir-fry for about 5 minutes. (Do not overcook—vegetables should be crisp.) Combine meat and vegetables; mix well.

Heat chicken stock, sugar, and soy sauce. Make a paste of cornstarch and a little cold water; stir into hot stock mixture. Cook, stirring constantly, until thickened. Pour over meat and vegetables. Allow time for flavors to blend before serving. Serve over chow mein noodles or rice. Makes 4 to 6 servings.

Sweet and Sour Pork

Noodles Romanoff

2	packages (8 ounces each) noodles
3	cups large curd cottage cheese
2	garlic cloves, mashed
2	teaspoons Worcestershire sauce
2	cups sour cream
½	cup milk
1	bunch green onions, chopped
½	teaspoon Tabasco sauce
1	cup grated Parmesan cheese

Cook noodles as package directs. Drain. Combine with other ingredients. Pour into buttered 2- or 3-quart casserole. Bake at 350 degrees until bubbly, about 15 minutes covered, then 15 minutes uncovered. Makes about 16 servings.

Note: Ingredients may be prepared ahead of time, then refrigerated. Allow an additional 15 minutes cooking time.

Pesto Sauce

1	cup parsley, packed
1 or 2	cloves garlic
1	teaspoon grated Parmesan cheese
1	teaspoon salt
½	cup olive oil

Blend all ingredients in blender until smooth. Split small loaf French bread lengthwise and spread with sauce. Broil until bubbly. For spaghetti sauce, add 2 tablespoons Pesto Sauce to meat sauce recipe.

Thyme-on-Your-Hands Chicken

Lion House Chicken

2	cups bread crumbs
5 to 6	cups cubed bread for stuffing
1	medium yellow onion, diced
3	stalks celery, diced
1	cup sliced fresh mushrooms
1	cup butter
1	tablespoon rubbed sage
3	cups chicken stock
	Salt and pepper to taste
8 to 10	boneless, skinless chicken breasts (7 ounces each)

Toast bread cubes in oven at 300 degrees until crisp and lightly browned. Sauté onion, celery, and mushrooms in butter until onion is translucent. Add sage and chicken stock and bring to a low boil. Season with salt and pepper to taste. In large bowl, toss hot mixture with bread cubes, adding enough liquid to make cubes soft but not soggy. Divide stuffing mixture into 8 to 10 equal parts.

Place each chicken breast between sheets of plastic wrap and pound to an even ½-inch thick. Bread one side of each chicken breast with crumbs, and hold chicken, breaded side down, in one hand. Put stuffing on top of the breast; fold over and secure with toothpicks. Bake at 350 degrees until cooked thoroughly, about 15 to 20 minutes. Test chicken with meat thermometer; internal temperature should be 155 degrees. Makes 8 to 10 servings.

Honey Dijon Sauce for Chicken

½	cup honey
⅓	cup Dijon mustard
2	cups mayonnaise

Mix honey, mustard, and mayonnaise together and chill. When chicken is cooked, drizzle sauce over hot chicken and serve.

Thyme-on-Your-Hands Chicken

1	chicken (4 or 5 pounds), quartered or whole
1	lemon
2	tablespoons fresh thyme leaves, *or* 1 tablespoon dry thyme leaves
	Kosher salt
	Cracked black pepper

Place whole chicken or quarters in lightly oiled roasting pan large enough that pieces do not touch. Squeeze juice of one lemon over chicken and leave lemon peel in pan. Rub thyme leaves over chicken. Sprinkle with salt and pepper. Roast at 350 degrees until chicken is cooked thoroughly, about 30 to 45 minutes. Serves 4.

Easy Chicken Bake

	Salt
	Garlic salt
	Paprika
6	chicken breasts
1	can (10½ ounces) cream of mushroom soup
1	cup cream, *or* ¾ cup evaporated milk
	Chopped parsley

Mix salt, garlic salt, and paprika. Thoroughly rub mixture into chicken pieces. Place chicken in one layer in shallow baking dish or pan. Dilute soup with cream and pour over chicken; sprinkle with parsley. Bake uncovered at 350 degrees for 1 1/2 hours. Makes 6 servings.

Baked Chicken Supreme

4	whole chicken breasts, halved
1/4	cup shortening
1	small garlic clove
1/3	cup chopped onion
1½	teaspoons salt
½	teaspoon sugar
½	teaspoon oregano (optional)
1/4	cup flour
1	cup tomato juice
1	can (about 10½ ounces) tomato soup
1	cup sour cream
1/4	cup milk
2	tablespoons grated Parmesan cheese
	Hot cooked rice

Brown chicken breasts in shortening, using more shortening if needed. Remove from frying pan and place in 9x9-inch baking dish. Pour off all but 2 tablespoons drippings. Add garlic and onion to skillet; cover and cook until soft but not brown, about 5 minutes. Blend in salt, sugar, oregano, and flour. Add tomato juice and tomato soup; heat to boiling, stirring constantly. Remove from heat and blend in sour cream. Stir vigorously. Add enough milk to thin sauce a little. Add Parmesan cheese. Pour over chicken in baking dish. Cover and bake at 325 degrees for about 45 minutes, or until meat is fork tender. Serve with cooked rice. Makes 8 servings.

Note: Skinned and boned breasts are best, but unskinned, unboned pieces may be used. Or use all pieces from one chicken, or pieces desired from two chickens.

Chicken Royale

4	whole chicken breasts, halved
2	tablespoons butter
1/4	cup chopped onion
1/4	pound fresh mushrooms
2	tablespoons flour
1	cup light cream
1	cup sour cream
1	teaspoon lemon juice
8	slices cooked ham

| ½ | of small package stuffing mix, made according to package directions, *or* make 2 cups of your own stuffing, using any favorite recipe |

Skin and bone each chicken breast half. Using a meat mallet or rolling pin, flatten each piece, skinned side down, between pieces of plastic wrap to about 1/8-inch thickness. In large frying pan, melt butter; cook onion and mushrooms, covered, until soft but not brown, about 10 minutes. Remove from pan and reserve. In same pan, brown flattened chicken breasts; add more butter, or cooking oil, if needed. Remove chicken pieces from pan and reserve.

Add flour to pan drippings and blend well. Gradually add light cream and sour cream. Heat well but do not boil, stirring constantly until mixture thickens. Add reserved onion and mushrooms, and lemon juice. Adjust seasonings to taste.

Grease a 9x13-inch baking dish. Cut ham slices to fit chicken breasts, and place ham slices in baking dish. Top each ham slice with about 1/4 cup stuffing; then cover with a chicken piece. Pour sauce mixture over all. Bake at 325 degrees for about half an hour, or until hot and bubbly and chicken is fork tender. Makes 8 servings.

Santa Fe Chicken

1	pound cream cheese
1	cup green chilies
8 to 12	chicken breasts (7 ounces each), boneless, skinless, pounded flat or butterflied
3	cups cornflake crumbs

Mix cream cheese and chilies until soft. Bread one side of each breast with crumbs. Holding breaded side down in your hand, place one heaping tablespoon cream cheese mixture on chicken and wrap chicken around mixture. Bake at 350 degrees until chicken is done, about 20 to 25 minutes. Makes 8 to 12 servings.

Chicken and Broccoli Bake

4   chicken breast halves

3   packages (10 ounces each) frozen broccoli, cooked according to package directions, *or* 2 pounds fresh broccoli, well trimmed and cooked until tender-crisp

1   can (10½ ounces) cream of chicken soup

½   cup milk

¼   cup mayonnaise

¼   cup salad dressing (such as Miracle Whip®)

1   cup grated cheddar cheese

1   teaspoon lemon juice

½   cup bread crumbs

¼   cup grated Parmesan cheese

2   tablespoons butter or margarine, cut into small pieces

Cook chicken breasts in water just to cover for about 30 minutes. Remove chicken; cool, remove bones and skin, and dice meat.

Coat 9x9-inch pan with nonstick cooking spray. Layer broccoli in bottom of pan; place chicken pieces on top of broccoli. Mix soup, milk, mayonnaise, salad dressing, cheddar cheese, and lemon juice. Spread on top of chicken. Sprinkle with bread crumbs and cheese, and top with butter or margarine. Bake at 350 degrees for 30 minutes or 20 minutes on high in microwave. Makes 5 to 6 servings.

Orange Chicken

½   cup flour

2   teaspoons salt

¼   teaspoon pepper

6 to 8   chicken breasts

⅓   cup butter, melted

1   onion, thinly sliced

6   ounces frozen orange juice concentrate

1   juice can water

¼   cup brown sugar

½   teaspoon nutmeg

2   tablespoons cornstarch

Combine flour, salt, and pepper in plastic bag. Add chicken pieces and shake to coat well. Brush each piece with butter. Place chicken pieces in baking pan, skin side up. Bake at 375 degrees for 40 minutes. Remove chicken to 2-quart casserole and spread onions generously over surface. Combine orange juice, water, brown sugar, nutmeg, and cornstarch. Pour over chicken. Cover with foil and bake at 325 degrees for half an hour or until fork tender. Makes 6 to 8 servings.

Chicken Cordon Bleu

4   whole chicken breasts, halved

8   thin slices cooked ham

4   slices Swiss cheese, cut into strips about 1½ inches long and ⅓-inch thick

   Salt

   Pepper

   Thyme or rosemary

¼   cup melted butter or margarine

½   cup cornflake crumbs

   Cordon Bleu Sauce (below)

Skin and bone chicken breast halves. Place each half between sheets of plastic wrap, skinned side down, and pound with meat mallet to about ⅛-inch thickness.

On each ham slice place a strip of cheese; sprinkle lightly with seasonings. Roll ham and cheese jelly-roll style, then roll each chicken breast with ham and cheese inside. Tuck in ends and seal well. (Tie rolls if necessary, or fasten edges with toothpicks.) Dip each roll in melted butter, then roll in cornflake crumbs, turning to thoroughly coat each roll. Place rolls in 9x13-inch baking dish. Bake uncovered at 400 degrees for about 40 minutes, or until chicken is golden brown. Serve with Cordon Bleu Sauce, if desired. Makes 6 to 8 servings.

Cordon Bleu Sauce

1   can (10½ ounces) cream of chicken soup

½   cup sour cream

   Juice of 1 lemon (about ⅛ cup)

Blend ingredients and heat. Serve over chicken rolls, if desired. Makes about 2 cups, or eight ¼-cup servings.

Chicken Alabam

Chicken Alabam

8   pieces chicken
⅓   cup flour
½   teaspoon paprika
½   teaspoon salt
    Dash pepper
    Dash thyme
5   tablespoons butter
¼   cup onion, chopped
1   cup chicken stock, *or* 2 chicken bouillon
    cubes, *or* 1½ teaspoons chicken soup
    base granules and 1 cup water

½   cup light cream
¼   teaspoon lemon juice
2   tablespoons pimiento

Dredge chicken pieces with mixture of flour, paprika, salt, pepper, and thyme. Brush chicken with 3 tablespoons melted butter and brown in oven, or shake off excess flour and sauté chicken in about 3 tablespoons cooking oil.

Sauté onion lightly in 2 tablespoons butter for 5 minutes. Stir in excess flour from dredging chicken. Add soup stock; cook and stir until thickened. Add light cream; cook until smooth and thick. Add lemon juice, then pimiento; blend well. Pour sauce over chicken in 2- to 3-quart casserole; cover and bake at 325 degrees for 1¼ hours, or until chicken is fork tender. Serve over cooked rice. Makes 4 to 5 servings, or 8 servings if only chicken breasts are used (a half breast for each serving).

Chicken and Cashews

4	chicken breast halves
1	teaspoon sugar
4	tablespoons cornstarch
½	teaspoon salt
¼	cup soy sauce
1	teaspoon vinegar
1	teaspoon Worcestershire sauce
3	tablespoons salad oil
2	cups hot chicken stock
2	teaspoons lemon juice
½	cup cashews
	Cooked rice

Bone and skin chicken breasts. Cover chicken bones and skin with cold water. Bring to a boil slowly and simmer for ½ hour or more. (Add a few slices of onion, carrot, and celery to improve flavor of the stock.) Strain and cool stock. Remove fat from surface.

Cut raw chicken into bite-sized pieces. Combine sugar, 2 tablespoons cornstarch, salt, soy sauce, vinegar, and Worcestershire sauce. Dredge chicken pieces in this mixture. Drain and save remaining mixture. In frying pan or wok, stir-fry chicken in hot oil until lightly browned and tender, about 10 minutes. Remove chicken from oil; drain excess oil from pan. Add remaining cornstarch and mixture drained from dredged chicken. Blend well, then add chicken stock to pan and bring to a boil, stirring constantly. Cook until thickened. Add lemon juice, then chicken pieces, and reheat. Do not boil. Adjust seasonings to taste. Add cashews. Serve over hot rice. Makes 4 to 5 servings.

Note: Chicken soup base or canned chicken stock may be used. Add water to desired consistency, if needed.

Quiche Lorraine

1	9-inch unbaked pie crust
1	cup (4 ounces) shredded Swiss cheese
6	slices bacon, cooked and crumbled
1	cup ham, minced
2	green onions, sliced and chopped
½	green pepper, chopped
5	eggs, slightly beaten
1	cup half-and-half
⅛	teaspoon grated lemon peel
½	teaspoon salt
⅓	teaspoon dry mustard

Arrange cheese, bacon, and ham in bottom of unbaked pie crust. Sprinkle with green onions and green pepper. In medium bowl combine eggs, half-and-half, lemon peel, salt, and dry mustard. Pour evenly over cheese mixture. Bake at 325 degrees for 45 minutes or until set. Remove from heat and let stand about 10 minutes before serving. Makes 6 servings.

Chicken Taco Pie

1	cup chopped onion
2	tablespoons cooking oil
2	tablespoons taco seasoning (or to taste)
1¾	tablespoons chili powder
1	teaspoon salt
¼	teaspoon pepper
3	cans (10½ ounces each) cream of mushroom soup
1½	cups sour cream
3	cups cubed cooked chicken
6 to 8	tortillas
1	cup Monterey Jack cheese, shredded

In skillet, cook onion in oil until tender but not brown. Add seasonings, cream of mushroom soup, and sour cream; heat and stir until smooth and warm. Add chicken. Grease 2- to 3-quart flat casserole and cover bottom of pan with torn-up oiled tortillas. Spread half the chicken mixture on tortillas. Top with additional oiled tortillas, then cover with remaining filling. Sprinkle with shredded cheese. Bake at 350 degrees until hot and bubbly. Makes 6 to 8 servings.

Parmesan Ranch Chicken

Parmesan Ranch Chicken

½ cup cornflake crumbs
½ cup grated Parmesan cheese
1½ ounces dry ranch dressing mix
6 boneless chicken breasts
¾ cup shredded Parmesan cheese
26 ounces marinara or spaghetti sauce

In shallow bowl, combine cornflake crumbs, ½ cup Parmesan cheese and ranch mix. Coat both sides of chicken with mix. Place in 9x13-inch pan sprayed with nonstick cooking spray. Spray tops of chicken with nonstick cooking spray to keep moist. Bake at 350 degrees for 25 to 30 minutes. Just prior to serving sprinkle with remaining Parmesan. Heat marinara sauce and serve over cooked pasta and chicken. Serves 6.

Triple Divan

2 packages (10 ounces each) frozen broccoli spears, or 2 pounds fresh broccoli
¾ pound cooked ham (8 serving-size slices)
¾ pound sliced cooked turkey breast, or 1 whole chicken breast, sliced
½ pound cooked shrimp
1 can (10½ ounces) cream of chicken soup
¾ cup mayonnaise
2 teaspoons curry powder
1 cup cream
1 cup evaporated milk
3 tablespoons lemon juice
2 tablespoons butter or margarine
2 cups soft buttered bread crumbs
½ pound (2 cups) finely shredded sharp cheese

Cook broccoli according to package directions. Be careful not to overcook. Or trim stems from fresh broccoli, wash, then cook in boiling salted water until just tender-crisp. Drain and arrange broccoli, in serving sizes, in 2- to 3-quart shallow baking dish. Arrange ham slices, then turkey slices, then shrimp over broccoli.

Combine soup, mayonnaise, curry, cream, evaporated milk, and lemon juice. Heat and stir until mixture is smooth and warm. Pour sauce over meat combination. Melt butter in frying pan. Add bread crumbs and stir until all are buttery and slightly brown. Add shredded cheese to crumb mixture. Combine well, then spread over sauce in baking dish. Bake at 350 degrees until sauce is hot and bubbly and crumbs are crispy and golden, about half an hour. Makes 8 servings.

Note: 2 cups whole milk may be used in place of cream and evaporated milk.

Apricot Chicken

2 tablespoons cornstarch
2 cups apricot nectar
1 envelope dry onion soup mix
2 frying chickens, cut up, or 8 chicken breasts

In saucepan, mix cornstarch in small amount of apricot nectar. Add remaining nectar and onion soup mix. Heat and stir until sauce thickens. Pour over chicken pieces that have been washed and dried and arranged in 9x13-inch baking dish. Bake covered at 350 degrees for 30 minutes. Uncover and bake about 30 minutes or until chicken is tender. Baste several times with sauce. Makes 8 servings.

Quick Chicken à la King

½ cup diced green pepper
½ tablespoon butter or margarine
1 can (10½ ounces) cream of mushroom or cream of chicken soup
1¼ cups milk
3 cups chicken, cooked and cubed
1 tablespoon pimiento, chopped
Dash pepper

Cook green pepper in butter until tender. Add soup; stir to blend. Gradually add milk; gently stir in remaining ingredients. Heat until sauce is bubbling and flavors are blended. Serve in patty shells, or on toast, rice, Chinese noodles, or biscuits. Makes eight ¾-cup servings.

Chicken à la King

Ingredients	12 servings	24 servings	36 servings
Shortening	½ cup	1 cup	1½ cups
Mushrooms, sliced	1½ cups	3 cups	4½ cups
Onions, chopped	¾ tablespoon	1½ tablespoons	2¼ tablespoons
Flour	6 tablespoons	¾ cup	1 cup plus 2 tablespoons
Chicken stock or consommé*	3 cups	6 cups	9 cups
Milk	2 cups	1 quart	1½ quarts
Chicken, cooked, cubed	4 cups**	8 cups**	12 cups**
Green pepper, chopped	½ cup	1 cup	1½ cups
Pimientos, chopped	½ cup	1 cup	1½ cups
Lemon juice	2 tablespoons	4 tablespoons	5 to 6 tablespoons
*or use chicken soup base,	¼ cup	½ cup	¾ cup
plus water	3 cups	6 cups	9 cups

** One pound cooked, cubed chicken equals about 3 cups.

Melt shortening in large saucepan or Dutch oven; add mushrooms and onions, and cook until lightly browned. Stir in flour and blend well. Gradually add stock and milk, stirring constantly. Cook until mixture thickens and comes to a boil. Fold in remaining ingredients. Serve on toast or rice, or in patty shells. Each serving is about ⅔ cup.

Bread Stuffing

Ingredients	For 4-pound chicken	For 12- to 16-pound turkey
Butter or margarine	⅓ cup	1 cup
Chopped onion	3 to 4 tablespoons	¾ to 1 cup
Finely chopped celery (optional)	¾ to 1 cup	2 cups
Stale bread cubes (¼- to ½-inch)	1 quart	3 to 4 quarts
Salt	1 teaspoon	1 tablespoon
Pepper	⅛ teaspoon	¼ teaspoon
Poultry seasoning	½ teaspoon	1½ teaspoons

Heat butter in large skillet; add onion and celery and cook until transparent but not brown, about 10 minutes. Add bread cubes and seasonings. Heat until bread cubes are lightly browned and butter is absorbed, stirring constantly.

Note: This recipe produces a somewhat dry and crumbly stuffing. For a moister stuffing, add ⅓ to 1 cup chicken or turkey stock or water. Adjust seasonings to taste.

Hawaiian Chicken

4 to 6	chicken breasts
	Flour
	Salt
	Cooking oil
1	can (15½ ounces) pineapple chunks
½	cup honey
2	tablespoons cornstarch
¾	cup cider vinegar
1	tablespoon soy sauce
¼	teaspoon ginger
1	chicken bouillon cube
1	green pepper, cut in ¼-inch strips

Roll chicken pieces in flour and sprinkle with salt. Brown in oil. Drain pineapple; reserve pineapple chunks, and pour juice into measuring cup. Add water to make 1½ cups. Add honey, cornstarch, vinegar, soy sauce, ginger, and bouillon cube; bring to a boil. Cook 2 minutes, stirring constantly. Pour over chicken pieces in 2-quart baking dish. Bake uncovered at 350 degrees for 20 minutes. Add pineapple chunks and green pepper; bake 5 minutes longer. Serve with cooked rice. Makes 4 to 6 servings.

Turkey Tetrazzini

8	ounces spaghetti, broken in pieces
5	tablespoons butter or margarine
6	tablespoons flour
3	cups chicken or turkey broth
1	cup light cream
1	teaspoon salt
	Pepper
1	cup fresh or canned mushrooms, including liquid
5	tablespoons minced green peppers
3	cups cooked turkey, cubed
½	cup grated Parmesan cheese
½	cup shredded Cheddar cheese

Cook spaghetti in boiling salted water until just tender (do not overcook). Melt butter; blend in flour. Stir broth into flour mixture. Add cream. Cook until mixture thickens and bubbles. Add salt and pepper, cooked spaghetti, mushrooms, green peppers, and cooked turkey. Turn into individual baking dishes or into 2- to 3-quart flat casserole. Sprinkle with cheeses. Bake at 350 degrees for about 30 minutes or until bubbly and lightly browned. Makes 8 servings.

Hawaiian Chicken

Halibut au Gratin

Broiled Fish Steaks or Fillets

- 8 fish steaks or fillets, washed well in cold running water
  Salt
  Paprika
- ¼ cup lemon juice
- ½ cup melted butter or margarine
- ¼ cup chopped parsley

Place fillets or steaks on well-greased baking sheet. Sprinkle with salt and paprika. Drip lemon juice and butter generously over fish. Broil about 6 inches from heat for about 10 minutes for each 1 inch of thickness, basting once with lemon and butter. When fish is firm and flakes easily, remove from broiler. Baste again with lemon and butter; garnish with parsley and serve immediately. Makes 8 servings.

Lemon Fish Bake

- 8 fish fillets, large enough for 1 serving each, washed well in cold running water
  Salt
- 5 tablespoons butter or margarine
- 1 lemon, thinly sliced
- ¼ to ½ cup sour cream
- ½ cup Cheddar cheese, shredded
  Lemon Sauce (below)

Place fillets in single layer in shallow buttered baking dish. Salt each fillet lightly, then top with about 2 teaspoons of melted butter. Cover with foil. Bake at 450 degrees until fish flakes easily with a fork. Do not overcook, or fish will be dry. Allow about 10 minutes baking time for each inch of thickness. When fish is baked, drain off part of liquid. Cover fish with Lemon Sauce. Serve each fillet topped with thin slice of lemon, dollop of sour cream, and shredded cheese. Makes 8 servings.

Lemon Sauce

- 1 tablespoon cornstarch
- 1 tablespoon butter or margarine
- 1½ cups water
- ¼ cup lemon juice

Make paste of cornstarch and butter. Bring water and lemon juice to a boil. Stir in cornstarch paste and cook until thickened. Use about 2 tablespoons sauce on each fillet.

Creamy Baked Halibut Steaks

- 4 halibut steaks, about ¾-inch thick
  Salt
  Pepper
- ¾ cup thick sour cream
- ¼ cup dry bread crumbs
- ¼ teaspoon garlic salt
- 1½ teaspoons chopped chives, fresh or frozen
- ⅓ cup grated Parmesan cheese
- 1 teaspoon paprika

Place steaks close together in shallow buttered baking dish; sprinkle with salt and pepper. Mix together sour cream, bread crumbs, garlic salt, and chives; spread over steaks. Sprinkle with Parmesan cheese and paprika. Bake uncovered at 400 degrees for 15 to 20 minutes, or until fish flakes with a fork. Makes 4 large or 8 small servings.

Halibut au Gratin

1 to 1½   pounds halibut
2 to 3   tablespoons each chopped onion, celery, carrot
¼   teaspoon salt
6   tablespoons butter or margarine
6   tablespoons flour
½   teaspoon salt
⅛   teaspoon white pepper
2½   cups milk
½   cup grated Parmesan cheese
2   cups shredded sharp Cheddar cheese
¼   cup chopped pimiento (optional)

In large frying pan, place halibut pieces in single layer; spread with chopped onion, celery, and carrot. Add ¼ teaspoon salt to small amount of water (about ½ cup) and pour into pan with fish. Cover and steam gently until fish flakes easily with fork, about 20 minutes. Turn fish after about 10 minutes. Remove fish from pan, scrape off vegetables, and when cool enough to handle, remove skin and bones; break fish into large chunks.

In the meantime, make a white sauce: Melt butter in small saucepan. Add flour, salt, and pepper; stir over medium heat until mixture foams. Add milk; stir occasionally until sauce is thick and smooth. Pour half the sauce into 2-quart casserole or 9x9-inch shallow baking dish. Layer fish chunks over sauce, then Parmesan cheese, then Cheddar cheese. Cover with remaining white sauce. Sprinkle with chopped pimiento. Bake at 350 degrees for about 30 minutes or until hot and bubbly. Do not overcook or fish will be tough and dry. Makes 6 servings.

Baked Salmon Steaks

6   salmon steaks, about ¾-inch thick, washed well in cold running water
⅓   cup melted butter
3   tablespoons fresh lemon juice (or more to taste)
½   teaspoon salt

Arrange salmon steaks in single layer in shallow, greased baking pan. Combine butter, lemon juice, and salt; spoon over steaks. Bake uncovered at 350 degrees for 15 to 20 minutes, or until fish flakes easily with fork. Remove salmon to warm serving platter; keep warm. Pour pan drippings into warm serving dish; add more lemon juice if desired. Pass sauce to spoon over salmon. Makes 6 servings.

Variations for Salmon Steaks

Honey Garlic
1   cup honey
3   cloves garlic
1   tablespoon soy sauce

Place ingredients in food processor and blend until garlic is well minced. Warm sauce. Brush over salmon steaks prior to baking.

Dill Lemon Pepper
1   tablespoon dill weed
2   teaspoons lemon pepper
  Butter

Mix together and sprinkle over salmon steaks; then place thin pats of butter on top of each steak prior to baking.

Salmon Tetrazzini

1   can (15½ ounces) salmon, skin removed
½   pound mushrooms, sliced
2   cloves garlic, minced
½   cup chopped green onions
¼   cup butter or margarine
¼   cup flour
1   cup chicken broth
1½   cups half-and-half
2   tablespoons lemon juice
½   teaspoon salt
⅛   teaspoon pepper
¼   cup grated Parmesan cheese
8   ounces spaghetti, cooked
3   tablespoons grated Parmesan cheese
  Lemon slice and parsley for garnish (if desired)

Salmon Steaks and Rice Pilaf

Drain and flake salmon, reserving liquid. Sauté mushrooms, garlic, and green onions in butter or margarine. Blend in flour. Gradually add chicken broth, half-and-half, lemon juice, and reserved salmon liquid. Cook, stirring constantly, until thickened and smooth. Add seasonings, ¼ cup grated Parmesan cheese, and salmon. Combine with spaghetti. Adjust seasonings to taste.

Turn into buttered 2½-quart casserole. Sprinkle with 3 tablespoons grated Parmesan cheese. Bake at 375 degrees for 20 to 25 minutes, until bubbly and slightly browned. Garnish with slice of lemon and sprig of parsley. Makes 6 to 8 servings.

Note: May be prepared in advance and refrigerated or frozen.

Shrimp Creole with Rice

2½ tablespoons butter or margarine
½ cup chopped green pepper
⅓ cup chopped green onions, including
   tops
1 cup chopped celery
2 tablespoons flour
⅛ teaspoon paprika
2 cups reserved tomato liquid, heated
1 can (1 pound 12 ounces) whole tomatoes,
   drained (reserve liquid)

1 small bay leaf
2 cans (5 ounces each) shrimp, drained, or
   1½ pounds fresh shrimp, cooked
1 tablespoon chopped parsley, or ¾ teaspoon dry parsley flakes
   Salt to taste
   Cooked rice

Melt butter in large frying pan or Dutch oven.
Sauté green pepper, green onions, and celery until
soft but not brown, 5 to 10 minutes on low heat.
Add flour and paprika; blend well. Add hot

Shrimp Creole with Rice

tomato liquid; cook and stir until smooth and thick. Add whole tomatoes and bay leaf. Cover and simmer 30 minutes. Add shrimp and continue cooking until shrimp is heated, about 5 minutes. Add parsley. Adjust seasonings to taste. Serve immediately over hot cooked rice. Makes 6 servings.

Seafood Newburg

¼	cup minced onion
¼	cup minced green pepper (optional)
1	cup butter
1	cup flour
¼	cup chopped pimiento (optional)
1	tablespoon paprika
1	teaspoon salt
¼	teaspoon white pepper
	Dash cayenne
4	cups milk, heated
1	cup light cream
2	tablespoons lemon juice
4	cups cooked seafood and fish*
	Pastry shells, cooked rice, or crisp toast

Make a thick white sauce: In top of 3- or 4-quart double boiler placed over medium heat, sauté onion and green pepper in butter, covered, until soft but not brown, about 5 minutes. Blend in flour and seasonings. Add hot milk and stir until mixture is very thick. Add part of cream, to desired consistency. Place pan over boiling water. Cover and cook for about 10 minutes. Add lemon juice, seafood, and fish. Add more cream if necessary. Adjust seasonings to taste. Serve in pastry shells or over hot cooked rice or buttered toast. Makes about 2 quarts, or about 10 servings.

Note: Sauce may be prepared and frozen up to a month in advance. Thaw overnight in refrigerator and reheat over boiling water, stirring frequently. If necessary, blend with whip or rotary beater until smooth. Then add seafood and lemon juice. Adjust seasonings to taste.

*Use at least 2 cups shrimp, crab meat, lobster or scallops. The remainder may be flaked cooked white fish, such as cod, haddock, halibut, or sole.

Shrimp-Cheese Fondue

3	cans (4½ ounces each) shrimp, deveined, or crab meat
3	cups white bread cubes
2	cups grated sharp Cheddar cheese
9	eggs, lightly beaten
4½	cups milk
1½	teaspoons salt
¾	teaspoon dry mustard
3	teaspoons minced onion
¼	teaspoon pepper

Layer shrimp, bread, and cheese in greased 2-quart casserole. Combine remaining ingredients and pour over layers in casserole. Bake at 350 degrees for about 1 hour, or until set. Makes 12 servings.

Hot Stuffed Avocado

4	large avocados, peeled and halved lengthwise (salt tops if desired)
¼	cup lemon juice
	Pinch garlic powder
½	teaspoon salt (optional)
¼	cup butter or margarine
2	tablespoons chopped green onion
½	teaspoon celery salt
	Dash cayenne pepper
¼	cup flour
2	cups light cream
1 to 2	cups cooked crab meat, shrimp, chicken, or turkey
1	cup sharp Cheddar cheese, grated

Roll outside of peeled avocados in lemon juice to preserve color. Sprinkle with garlic powder and salt. Remove pits from halved avocados; place avocados in large baking pan. In saucepan melt butter; add green onion, celery salt, and cayenne pepper; cook 5 minutes over medium heat. Blend in flour. Add cream and cook, stirring until thickened. Fold in seafood or poultry and ½ cup cheese. Adjust seasonings to taste. Ladle filling over avocados. Bake avocados at 350 degrees for 15 minutes. Remove from oven and arrange on serving plates. Top with remaining cheese. Serve immediately. Makes 8 servings.

Vegetables

German Green Beans

1 cup water
1 tablespoon vinegar
1 medium onion, finely chopped
2 pounds green beans, cleaned and cut into ½-inch pieces
½ teaspoon salt
2 tablespoons bacon drippings

In saucepan combine water, vinegar, and onion. Bring to a boil; add beans. Cover; simmer for about 20 minutes or until beans are tender. Add salt and bacon drippings. Cook uncovered over high heat for 5 minutes. Makes 6 to 8 servings.

Note: Two 1-pound cans canned green beans, drained, may be used. Use 1 cup liquid drained from beans in place of water.

Hungarian Green Beans

1½ pounds green beans
1½ cups boiling water
½ teaspoon salt
6 slices bacon, chopped
1 onion, finely chopped
2 tablespoons flour
1 tablespoon vinegar
⅔ cup sour cream

Trim ends of beans; break into 1-inch lengths. Place in saucepan with water and salt; bring to a boil. Cover; simmer for about 25 minutes.

In the meantime, cook bacon in skillet until crisp. Add onion; sauté until transparent. Stir in flour, then vinegar. Gradually stir in hot liquid from beans; cook, stirring, until creamy and smooth. Add beans. Stir in sour cream. Cover and let stand for 2 minutes before serving. Makes 6 servings.

Italian Green Beans

4 slices thick bacon
2 tablespoons bacon drippings
1 green onion, chopped
1 tablespoon chopped green pepper
1 can (16 ounces) green beans, drained
1 can (16 ounces) seasoned tomatoes
½ teaspoon salt

Sauté bacon in hot frying pan until cooked but not crisp. Remove from pan. Measure 2 tablespoons drippings into frying pan. Add onion and green pepper; cook until soft but not brown, about 5 minutes. Add green beans, seasoned tomatoes, salt, and bacon pieces. Stir; cover and simmer for 20 minutes. Makes 6 servings.

Green Beans Parisienne

2 cans (1 pound each) cut green beans, *or* 2 packages (10 ounces each) frozen green beans, or 1 pound fresh green beans, cooked
1 can (10½ ounces) cream of mushroom soup
½ cup water or milk
½ teaspoon Worcestershire sauce, or 1 teaspoon soy sauce
½ cup shredded Cheddar cheese

Drain canned beans, or cook frozen or fresh beans and drain well. Combine soup, water or milk, and Worcestershire sauce; stir until smooth. Combine soup mixture with green beans and pour into 2-quart baking dish. Top with shredded cheese. Bake at 350 degrees for 30 minutes, or until cheese melts and browns slightly. Makes 4 to 6 servings.

Italian Green Beans

Green Beans Parmesan

Ingredients	12 servings	25 servings
Bacon, diced	6 ounces	12 ounces
Onions, finely chopped	¾ cup	1½ cups
Green beans, canned, cut	6 cups	1 No. 10 can
Salt*	¼ teaspoon	¾ teaspoon
Cornflake crumbs	½ cup	1 cup (3 oz.)
Parmesan cheese, grated	½ cup	1 cup (4 oz.)

Fry bacon until crisp; remove from fat and drain. Cook onions in bacon fat until tender, stirring constantly. Drain off most of bacon fat. Heat green beans; drain well. Add bacon, onions, salt, cornflake crumbs, and cheese to green beans; toss lightly until thoroughly mixed. Serve immediately. Size of serving is about ½ cup.

*Amount of salt will depend on saltiness of beans.

Sesame Green Beans

1 pound fresh green beans

Wash green beans, snip ends, and cut into ¼- to ½-inch lengths. Cook in boiling salted water until just tender. Drain. Serve with hot Sesame-Soy Sauce (below). Makes 4 servings.

Sesame-Soy Sauce

1 tablespoon toasted sesame seeds
1 tablespoon soy sauce
2 tablespoons butter or margarine, melted

Combine ingredients and heat. Serve over green beans. Sauce is also good on cooked, well-drained spinach or asparagus.

South of the Border Beans

6 slices bacon
½ cup finely chopped onion
½ cup chopped celery
3 cups cooked green beans
1 can (8 ounces) tomato sauce
1 teaspoon Worcestershire sauce
Salt and pepper to taste
½ cup bread crumbs, buttered

Sauté bacon, onion, and celery together. Combine beans, tomato sauce, Worcestershire sauce, salt and pepper, and bacon mixture. Turn into greased 1½-quart casserole, and top with buttered crumbs. Bake uncovered at 375 degrees for 20 minutes. Makes 6 servings.

Baked Beans

2 cans (29 ounces each) pork and beans
2 large onions, chopped
2 large green peppers, chopped
1 cup catsup
1 cup brown sugar
2 teaspoons Worcestershire sauce
1 pound lean bacon, cut up and cooked till crisp, then drained

Combine ingredients well in 9x13-inch baking pan. Bake at 325 degrees for 2½ hours, covered with aluminum foil. Uncover and bake another 30 minutes. Makes 8 to 10 servings.

Lemon Carrots and Apples

12 medium-sized carrots, cut in thin slices
½ teaspoon salt
1 teaspoon grated lemon peel
¼ cup butter or margarine
2 large tart apples, peeled, cored, and cut in ⅛-inch slices
2 tablespoons chopped parsley

Place carrots in shallow 2-quart casserole. Sprinkle with salt and lemon peel; dot with butter. Bake covered at 375 degrees until almost tender, about 30 minutes. Stir in apples. Cover and bake 10 to 20 minutes more, or until apples are tender. Stir well just before serving, and sprinkle with parsley. Makes about 8 servings.

Pineapple Carrots

Pineapple Carrots

3	cups sliced carrots
1	cup pineapple chunks, unsweetened, canned or fresh
½	teaspoon seasoned salt
3	tablespoons orange juice
1	tablespoon butter or margarine

Place carrots, pineapple, salt, and orange juice in 1½-quart casserole. Dot with butter, and cover. Bake at 375 degrees for 45 to 55 minutes. Makes 4 servings.

Stewed Cabbage and Carrots

2	cups shredded carrots
1	cup boiling water
3	cups shredded cabbage
2	tablespoons butter or margarine
1	teaspoon salt

Cook carrots in boiling water until partly tender, about 5 minutes. Add cabbage and simmer uncovered for 10 minutes. Add butter and salt; cook five minutes. Most of liquid should be absorbed in cooking; serve without draining. Makes 6 servings.

Glazed Broccoli with Almonds

Savory Cabbage

1 medium head cabbage, shredded
½ teaspoon salt
  Water
2 tablespoons butter or margarine
1 teaspoon finely chopped green onion
¼ cup cream
  Pepper

Cook cabbage in salted boiling water to cover until just tender. Drain well. In large skillet, melt butter; add onion, and cook for about 5 minutes or until onion is soft but not brown. Add cabbage and mix well. Pour cream over cabbage, and sprinkle with pepper. Serve at once. Makes 4 to 6 servings.

Caraway Cabbage

½ cup chopped onion
2 tablespoons butter or margarine, melted
1 cup water
2 teaspoons sugar
1 teaspoon salt
1¼ teaspoons caraway seed
2 teaspoons white vinegar
½ large red cabbage

In large saucepan over medium heat, cook onion in butter until tender. Add water and remaining ingredients. Simmer covered 8 minutes or until cabbage is tender-crisp. Serve immediately. Makes about 6 servings.

Glazed Broccoli with Almonds

2 pounds broccoli, or 2 packages (10 ounces each) frozen broccoli
½ teaspoon salt
1 chicken bouillon cube
¾ cup hot water
¼ cup butter or margarine
¼ cup flour
1 cup light cream
2 tablespoons lemon juice
  Salt and pepper to taste
¼ cup grated Parmesan cheese
¼ cup slivered blanched almonds

Separate broccoli; trim stems and wash thoroughly. Add salt, and cook in boiling water for 6 minutes or until barely tender. Drain and arrange in 9x9-inch baking pan.

While broccoli is cooking, prepare sauce: Dissolve bouillon cube in ¾ cup hot water. Melt butter or margarine in saucepan; blend in flour. Gradually stir in cream and dissolved bouillon cube; cook over medium heat, stirring constantly, until thickened and smooth. Remove from heat and stir in lemon juice, salt, and pepper. Adjust seasonings to taste. Pour sauce over broccoli. Sprinkle with cheese and almonds. Bake at 375 degrees for 20 minutes or until golden brown. Makes 6 to 8 servings.

Broccoli with Mustard Sauce

3 pounds fresh broccoli, cleaned and heavy part of stems removed, or 3 packages (10 ounces each) frozen broccoli, cooked as directed on package
2 tablespoons finely chopped onion
½ cup butter or margarine
½ cup flour
1½ cups milk (part chicken stock, if desired)
3 tablespoons lemon juice
2 tablespoons prepared mustard
2 teaspoons sugar
1 teaspoon salt

Cook broccoli in boiling salted water until just tender-crisp. While broccoli cooks, sauté onion in butter until tender but not brown, about 5 minutes. Stir in flour, then gradually add milk. Cook and stir until smooth and thickened. Add remaining ingredients. Serve over well-drained hot broccoli. Makes 8 servings.

Company Cauliflower

2 teaspoons sesame seeds
1 medium head cauliflower
Dash salt
Dash pepper
1 cup sour cream
½ to 1 cup shredded Cheddar cheese

In shallow pan, toast sesame seeds on medium heat for 10 minutes or until browned, shaking pan occasionally. Rinse cauliflower and separate into small flowerets. Cook in 2-quart covered saucepan, in 1 inch boiling salted water, 8 to 10 minutes, or until tender; drain well. Place half the cauliflower in 1-quart casserole. Season with salt and pepper; spread with ½ cup sour cream and sprinkle with half the cheese; top with 1 teaspoon sesame seed. Repeat layers. Bake at 375 degrees for 15 minutes, or until heated through. Makes 6 servings.

Harvard Beets

½ cup vinegar
½ cup water
3 cups sliced cooked beets, drained (reserve liquid)
1 tablespoon cornstarch
1 teaspoon sugar
Dash ground cloves
Dash salt
1 tablespoon butter

Heat together vinegar, water, beet liquid, cornstarch, sugar, cloves, and salt. Stir until thickened. Add beets and butter; reheat. Makes 6 to 8 servings.

Beets and Onions

2 tablespoons butter or margarine
2 cups sliced pickled beets, drained
1 cup sliced thin onion rings
2 teaspoons sugar
½ teaspoon salt
Pepper

Melt butter; add beets and onion rings. Simmer covered for 15 minutes. Add seasonings. Makes 4 servings.

Crumb-Topped Baked Onions

18 to 20 small white boiling onions
1 chicken bouillon cube
¾ cup water
2 tablespoons melted butter or margarine
½ teaspoon sage
¼ teaspoon pepper
1½ teaspoons cornstarch
1 tablespoon water
¼ cup croutons, slightly crushed
2 tablespoons grated Parmesan cheese
1 tablespoon chopped parsley

Peel onions and arrange in single layer in 8- or 9-inch square baking dish. Crush bouillon cube, then stir in water and heat until cube is dissolved. Stir in melted butter, sage, and pepper. Pour over onions. Cover and bake at 350 degrees for about 1 hour or until tender when pierced. Transfer onions to heated serving dish; keep warm.

Pour cooking juices into small saucepan. Blend cornstarch and 1 tablespoon water. Stir cornstarch mixture into cooking juices and cook, stirring, until sauce boils and thickens. Pour over onions. Combine croutons, Parmesan cheese, and chopped parsley; sprinkle evenly over onions. Makes 4 to 6 servings.

Creamed Onions

2 to 3 pounds (18 to 24) small white onions, peeled
4 tablespoons butter or margarine
4 tablespoons flour
1 teaspoon salt
⅛ teaspoon pepper
2 cups milk

In medium saucepan, cook onions in boiling salted water for about 20 minutes or until tender (be careful not to overcook). Drain; return to saucepan. While onions cook, melt butter over low heat in small saucepan. Blend in flour, salt, and pepper; stir until bubbly. Stir in milk; continue cooking and stirring 1 minute, until sauce thickens and boils. Pour over drained onions; heat slowly until bubbly. Makes 6 to 8 servings.

Honeyed Onions

1	can (8 ounces) tomato sauce
½	cup honey
¼	cup butter or margarine
16	small, raw, whole peeled onions

In saucepan, combine tomato sauce, honey, and butter. Add onions and simmer slowly until tender. Let stand in syrup. Reheat (the more times the better) and serve. If syrup boils down, add a little water or tomato juice. Makes 4 servings.

Pineappled Sweet Potatoes

6	medium sweet potatoes or yams, cooked and peeled
⅓	cup sugar
⅓	cup brown sugar
¼	teaspoon salt
2	tablespoons cornstarch
½	cup pineapple juice
½	cup orange juice
1	can (13½ ounces) pineapple chunks, tidbits, or crushed pineapple, well drained
2	tablespoons butter

Cook sweet potatoes in boiling salted water until tender. Cut into thick slices; arrange in shallow baking dish. In heavy saucepan, stir and blend well sugars, salt, and cornstarch. In small saucepan, bring fruit juices to a boil; gradually add to sugar mixture. Cook and stir until thickened. Add pineapple and butter; pour over sweet potatoes. Serve immediately, or place in 350-degree oven just until bubbly hot. Makes 8 servings.

Yam and Apple Casserole

6	medium yams
3 or 4	apples, peeled, cored, and sliced
½	cup butter or margarine
2 to 3	tablespoons cornstarch
1	cup sugar
1	teaspoon salt
2	cups pineapple or orange juice
2	tablespoons lemon juice

Parboil yams about 20 minutes; cool. Peel and slice; place yam slices and apple slices in layers in buttered casserole. Melt butter in small saucepan. Add cornstarch, sugar, and salt; blend well. Add pineapple or orange juice; cook and stir until sauce thickens. Add lemon juice; pour sauce over yams and apples. Bake at 350 degrees for 1 hour. Makes 8 servings.

Potato Casserole

5	large potatoes
3	tablespoons butter or margarine, melted
1	can (10½ ounces) cream of chicken soup
1	cup sour cream
1	cup milk
3	tablespoons finely chopped green onions
¾	cup shredded sharp Cheddar cheese
¾	cup cornflake crumbs or dry bread crumbs
2	tablespoons butter or margarine, melted
3	tablespoons grated Parmesan cheese

Boil unpared potatoes until tender. Drain and peel; shred coarsely. Place in 2- or 3-quart casserole. Pour melted butter over potatoes. Mix together soup, sour cream, milk, green onions, and cheese. Pour evenly over potatoes. Do not mix. Toss crumbs with melted butter and Parmesan cheese; sprinkle on top of casserole. Bake at 325 degrees for 30 minutes. Makes 8 to 10 servings.

Potatoes in Sour Cream

2	pounds (about 6 medium) potatoes
2	tablespoons butter or margarine
1	medium onion, minced
¼	cup bread crumbs
¼	cup shredded sharp Cheddar cheese
2	eggs, slightly beaten
1	cup sour cream
½	teaspoon salt
⅛	teaspoon pepper

Scrub potatoes and cook in boiling salted water. Drain; peel and slice into 2-quart baking dish. Melt butter in skillet; add onion, and brown slightly. Add onion, bread crumbs, and cheese to potatoes. Beat eggs and stir into sour cream. Add salt and pepper. Pour over potatoes. Bake at 350 degrees for 15 to 20 minutes, until well-heated and slightly brown. Makes 6 servings.

Potatoes Au Gratin

12	medium-sized potatoes, cooked
6	tablespoons butter or margarine
6	tablespoons flour
½	teaspoon seasoned salt
1	teaspoon salt
½	teaspoon garlic salt
	Pepper to taste
¼	teaspoon dry mustard
4	cups milk, heated
2	cups shredded cheese

Dice cooked potatoes. Melt butter in saucepan and stir in flour and seasonings. Cook, stirring constantly, until mixture bubbles. Gradually add milk, and cook over low heat, stirring constantly until sauce thickens and boils. Stir in ¾ cup shredded cheese and diced potatoes. Turn into baking dish, top with rest of cheese, and bake at 375 degrees for about 15 minutes, until cheese melts and browns. Makes about 14 to 16 servings.

Rice Pilaf

2	tablespoons butter or margarine
1	cup uncooked rice
¼	cup minced onion
⅓	cup minced celery
3	cups hot chicken broth
2	tablespoons chopped parsley
¼	cup slivered almonds

Melt butter in hot frying pan. Add rice, onion, and celery; stir and cook until slightly brown. Add chicken broth. Cover and simmer on low heat until moisture has been absorbed and rice is tender. Add parsley and almonds just before serving. Toss lightly. Makes 8 half-cup servings.

Oriental Rice

Ingredients	10 servings	20 servings
Bacon	¼ pound	½ pound
Onions, diced	1 cup	2 cups
Carrots, diced	½ cup	1 cup
Celery, diced	¾ cup	1½ cups
Green pepper, diced	¼ cup	½ cup
Cooked meat, diced	2 cups	4 cups
Soy sauce	3 tablespoons	6 tablespoons
Cold cooked rice	3 cups	6 cups

In large skillet, cook bacon until crisp; remove from skillet. Add onions and stir-fry one minute. Add carrots and stir-fry one minute. Add celery and green pepper and stir-fry one minute. Add meat and soy sauce and heat through. Break up cold cooked rice. Stir gently into meat and vegetables, taking care that each grain of rice is coated with oil and liquids that have formed in the pan. Heat through; add crumbled bacon and serve immediately.

Almond Celery Casserole

4	cups celery, sliced diagonally
1	can (10 ounces) cream of celery soup
½	cup sour cream
1	cup water chestnuts, sliced
½	cup shredded sharp Cheddar cheese
½	cup slivered almonds
½	cup seasoned bread crumbs (stuffing mix)

Cook celery in lightly salted boiling water, just until tender-crisp. Drain well and add soup, sour cream, and water chestnuts. Pour into shallow 2-quart baking dish. Top with cheese, then almonds, then bread crumbs. Bake at 350 degrees for 30 minutes, or until hot and lightly browned. Makes 4 to 6 servings.

Chinese Spinach

- 1 pound fresh spinach
- 2 tablespoons salad oil
- 2 tablespoons soy sauce
- ½ teaspoon sugar
- 2 tablespoons finely chopped onion
- 1 can (8 ounces) water chestnuts, drained and sliced

Wash and pat spinach leaves dry; tear into bite-sized pieces. In large saucepan, simmer spinach with small amount of water for 3 minutes; drain thoroughly. Heat oil, soy sauce, and sugar in skillet; add spinach and onion. Cook and toss until spinach is well-coated, 2 to 3 minutes. Stir in water chestnuts. Makes 4 servings.

Vegetable Medley

Vegetable Medleys

- 2 medium carrots
- 3 small zucchini
- 3 ribs celery
  Water
- 2 tablespoons butter
  Salt and pepper to taste

Peel carrots; wash and clean zucchini and celery. Slice vegetables diagonally. Place ¼ inch water and butter in saucepan and bring to a boil. Add carrots and simmer covered for 4 minutes. Add celery and simmer an additional 2 minutes. Add zucchini and continue cooking for an additional 5 minutes, or until all vegetables are tender-crisp. Season to taste with salt and pepper. Serve at once, retaining remaining liquid in serving dish. Makes 4 servings.

Vegetable Medley 2

Combine cooked, sliced, small yellow summer squash with package of cooked green peas. Season with salt, pepper, and butter.

Vegetable Medley 3

Combine cauliflower, broccoli, and carrots. Season with salt, pepper, and butter.

Baked Summer Squash

- 4 medium-sized yellow crookneck squash
  Salt
- 1 small onion, finely chopped
- 2 tablespoons butter or margarine
- ½ cup cream
- ¼ cup saltine crackers, crushed
  Butter
  Soft bread crumbs

Slice squash and boil in salted water until tender. Drain well and mash. Sauté onion in butter until transparent but not brown, 5 to 10 minutes. Add to squash. Add cream and cracker crumbs. Pour into greased 1-quart casserole. Dot with butter and a few soft bread crumbs. Bake at 400 degrees for about half an hour, or until firm. Makes 4 to 6 servings.

Zucchini Italian

1	pound zucchini
1	clove garlic, sliced
1	tablespoon olive oil
1	large tomato, peeled and quartered
1½	teaspoons salt
½	teaspoon oregano
	Pepper to taste

Scrub zucchini with stiff brush and slice crosswise into thin slices. In 1½-quart pan, sauté garlic in oil 1 minute. Stir in zucchini and remaining ingredients; cover and cook over low heat 15 minutes. Makes 4 servings.

Stuffed Zucchini

3	medium zucchini
1	package (10 ounces) frozen spinach, cooked
2	tablespoons flour
½	cup milk
	Salt
⅓	cup shredded Cheddar cheese
3	strips bacon, cut in half

Trim off ends of zucchini; cook, drain, and cut in half lengthwise. Scoop out pulp; drain and chop pulp and add to cooked spinach. Blend flour and milk; cook and stir until thickened. Add spinach-zucchini mixture. Salt hollowed-out zucchini shells. Add creamed filling; top with cheese and bacon. Bake at 350 degrees for 20 minutes. Makes 6 servings, ½ zucchini each.

Cheese Sauce

3	tablespoons butter or margarine
3	tablespoons flour
1½	teaspoons prepared mustard
1½	cups milk
½	pound grated Cheddar cheese
½	teaspoon salt
1	dash hot pepper sauce
1	tablespoon onion juice
1	tablespoon Worcestershire sauce

Melt butter; add flour and mustard, and blend. Add milk; stir over medium heat until thick. Stir in cheese, salt, hot pepper sauce, onion juice, and Worcestershire sauce. Stir until thick. Remove from heat. Serve on cauliflower, broccoli, or cabbage. Makes enough for 8 to 10 servings.

Mock Hollandaise Sauce

¾	cup mayonnaise
¼	cup butter or margarine, softened
½	teaspoon salt
	Dash pepper
1	tablespoon lemon juice
1	teaspoon grated lemon rind (optional)

Blend mayonnaise, butter, salt, and pepper; cook over low heat until butter melts and mixture is hot and smooth. Add lemon juice and rind. Serve on asparagus, broccoli, or poached fish, or with any recipe calling for Hollandaise Sauce. Makes about 1 cup.

Lemon Sauce

2	egg yolks
1	cup sugar
2	tablespoons cornstarch
1	orange
	Lemon juice

Combine egg yolks and sugar in small heavy saucepan; add cornstarch. Squeeze juice from orange; add lemon juice to make 1 cup. Add juice to mixture in saucepan and mix well. Stir and cook until thick. Serve over broccoli. Makes about 1 cup.

Lion House Dinner Rolls

2	cups warm water (110 to 115 degrees)
⅔	cup nonfat dry milk (instant or non-instant)
2	tablespoons dry yeast
¼	cup sugar
2	teaspoons salt
⅓	cup butter, shortening, or margarine
1	egg
5 to 5½	cups all-purpose flour, or bread flour

In large bowl of electric mixer, combine water and milk powder; stir until milk dissolves. Add yeast, then sugar, salt, butter, egg, and 2 cups flour. Mix on low speed of mixer until ingredients are wet, then for 2 minutes at medium speed. Add 2 cups flour; mix on low speed until ingredients are wet, then for 2 minutes at medium speed. (Dough will be getting stiff and remaining flour may need to be mixed in by hand.) Add about ½ cup flour and mix again, by hand or mixer. Dough should be soft, not overly sticky, and not stiff. (It is not necessary to use the entire amount of flour.)

Scrape dough off sides of bowl and pour about one tablespoon of vegetable oil all around sides of bowl. Turn dough over in bowl so it is covered with oil. (This helps prevent dough from drying out.) Cover with plastic and allow to rise in warm place until double in size. Sprinkle cutting board or counter with flour and place dough on floured board. Roll out and cut rolls into desired shape and size. Place on greased (or parchment lined) baking pans. Let rise in warm place until rolls are double in size (about 1–1½ hours).

Bake at 375 degrees for 15 to 20 minutes or until browned. Brush with melted butter while hot. Makes 1 to 1½ dozen rolls.

Helpful Tips for Making Rolls

Always add flour gradually and keep dough as soft as you can handle.

It is not necessary to use the entire amount of flour listed on the recipe—add only enough flour to make a manageable dough.

A soft dough will produce a lighter roll.

To shorten dough's rising time, use one of these methods: (1) When dough is thoroughly mixed, oil bowl and cover dough with plastic. Fill sink or larger bowl with about 2 inches of hot water or enough water to come about half or three-fourths the way up outside of bowl. Place bowl of dough in bowl of water and allow to rise until double in size. (2) Just before mixing dough, turn oven on lowest possible temperature. When dough is thoroughly mixed, place in oiled bowl. Cover dough with plastic; place in oven, with pan of hot water on rack under dough. Turn oven off, shut oven door, and allow dough to rise until double in size. Shape or cut into desired rolls. Place rolls on greased or parchment-lined pans and allow to rise until double in size. Bake according to recipe.

Both quick-rise methods may be used for second rise after shaping and placing rolls in pans. For method 1, fill sink or bowl halfway with hot water, place pan of shaped rolls across hot water. Allow rolls to rise until double in size, and bake according to recipe. (Be sure pan will fit across water-filled sink or large bowl so that rolls do not fall in the water.) For method 2, reheat oven while shaping rolls. Place fresh pan of hot water in oven with pan of rolls. Turn oven off and shut door. Allow rolls to rise until half again the size they were when shaped. Remove from oven and

Lion House Dinner Rolls

preheat oven for baking. When rolls are double the size when shaped, bake according to recipe.

Brush top of rolls with butter when first taken from oven.

How to consistently make attractive, good-tasting rolls? *PRACTICE! PRACTICE! PRACTICE!*

Shaping Lion House Rolls

After allowing dough to rise until double in size, scrape dough out onto floured counter or cutting board. Turn dough over so it is floured on both sides, and gently flatten to about 1 inch thick. With rolling pin, roll out to a rectangle about 18 inches long, 8 inches wide, and ¼ of an inch thick. Brush with melted butter. With pizza cutter or very sharp knife, cut dough in half to make two strips about 4 inches wide. Make cuts through strips of dough every 2 inches, making about 18 pieces of dough.

Starting with short end, roll one piece of dough with butter on the inside. Place roll on parchment-lined pan with other short end down on the paper. Repeat with remaining pieces of dough. Be sure all rolls face the same direction on baking pan. Cover lightly with plastic wrap and allow to rise until double in size. Bake at 375 degrees for 15 to 18 minutes, or until light to medium golden brown. Brush tops of rolls with melted butter.

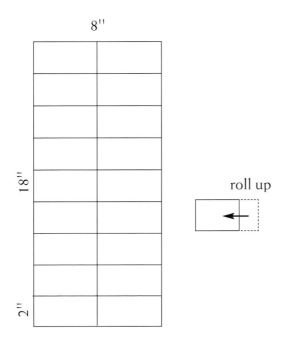

Bread Sticks

Prepare one recipe of Lion House roll dough. Roll dough in rectangle about ½-inch thick. Brush with melted butter; cut in desired widths and lengths (¾-inch wide and 4 to 5 inches long is ideal). Leave tops plain, or sprinkle with poppy seeds, sesame seeds, Parmesan cheese, or the following mixture:

1	teaspoon poppy seed
1	teaspoon sesame seed
½	teaspoon fennel seeds
½	teaspoon caraway seeds
⅛	teaspoon celery seed, or cumin, or dill seeds, or all three

Allow to rise until half again the size when rolled out. Bake at 375 degrees for about 10 minutes.

Lion House Raisin Bread

Prepare one recipe Lion House roll dough and add the following before final addition of flour:

2	cups raisins
1½	teaspoons yeast
¾	teaspoons cinnamon
¾	teaspoons nutmeg

Mix in ingredients while adding last amount of flour. Pour a little oil around edge of bowl and scrape down bowl. Turn dough over once in bowl so dough is covered with oil. Cover with plastic wrap and allow to rise until double in size. Shape into 2 loaves and place in large greased loaf pans. Allow to rise until dough is 1 inch above edge of pan. Bake at 350 degrees for 25 to 30 minutes, or until golden brown. Brush with melted butter after removing from oven; remove from pan and cool on wire rack.

Orange Rolls

Prepare one recipe of Lion House roll dough. Roll dough to rectangle about ¼-inch thick. Brush dough with orange butter and sprinkle ¼ cup sugar on top. With pizza cutter, cut 3½ inch strips on long side of rectangle. Starting at short side of rectangle, cut 2-inch strips of dough. Roll up strips, starting with narrow edge. Place on lightly greased baking sheet with cut edge flat on baking sheet. Allow to rise until double in size. Bake at 375 degrees for 12 to 15 minutes, until light golden brown. Remove from oven and brush with melted butter. Allow to cool about 10 to 15 minutes; drizzle with the icing.

Orange Butter

½ cup butter, melted
Zest of 2 oranges

Stir together melted butter and orange zest

Icing

1½ cups powdered sugar
2 tablespoons orange juice, squeezed from zested oranges above
2 to 4 tablespoons heavy cream, or 2 tablespoons half-and-half

Place powdered sugar and orange juice in bowl; add half the amount of heavy cream. With spoon or mixer, mix until smooth. If icing is too thick, add more cream a little at a time. The hotter the rolls are when frosted, the thicker the frosting needs to be (add 1 to 2 teaspoons of orange zest, if desired).

Caramel Rolls

Prepare one recipe of Lion House roll dough; allow to rise once. Divide dough into three equal parts, using 2 parts for the following recipe. Place third part in greased loaf pan and let rise; bake at 375 degrees for about 35 minutes.

2 parts Lion House roll dough
½ cup melted butter
1 cup brown sugar
1 large package (6 ounces) vanilla pudding mix (not instant)
3 tablespoons milk
½ teaspoon cinnamon
Cinnamon-sugar

Coat 9x13-inch pan or large Bundt pan with non-stick vegetable spray. Tear 1 part of dough into small pieces and drop randomly in bottom of pan. Melt butter and add remaining ingredients. Stir until well blended. Pour ⅔ of this mixture over the dough pieces in pan. Tear second piece of dough into pan to fill in empty spots. Pour remaining sauce over dough pieces; sprinkle with cinnamon-sugar. Cover with plastic wrap and allow to rise in warm place until double in size, 45 minutes to 1 hour. Bake at 375 degrees for 30 minutes. Allow to cool 10 minutes, then invert onto large platter.

Note: Rhodes frozen dough may be substituted for Lion House dough. Allow 2 loaves of frozen dough to thaw; use one loaf for bottom layer and one for top layer.

Rich Corn Bread

1 cup flour
1 cup cornmeal
1 teaspoon salt
4 teaspoons baking powder
4 eggs
½ cup sour cream
1 can (1 pound) cream-style corn
2 tablespoons salad oil
¾ cup grated cheese

Sift dry ingredients together; set aside. Beat eggs until light; add sour cream, corn, and salad oil. Stir in dry ingredients and beat well. Pour into well-greased 8x4-inch loaf pan or 8x8-inch square pan. Sprinkle with grated cheese. Bake at 400 degrees for 30 minutes.

Rich Corn Bread

Whole Wheat Bread

1	package (1 tablespoon) dry yeast
3	cups lukewarm water
1	cup oatmeal
¼	cup molasses
6	tablespoons nonfat dry milk
6	tablespoons shortening, softened
5½	cups whole wheat flour
1½	tablespoons salt
2	cups white flour

Instructions for Mixing with Electric Mixer

Soften yeast in 3 cups lukewarm water in large mixing bowl. Add remaining ingredients and beat until dough forms a ball and leaves sides of bowl (part of flour may need to be mixed in by hand). Remove beaters, cover bowl, and let dough rise for 1 hour in warm place away from drafts. Mix down and mold into 2 loaves. Place in greased loaf pans and let rise until about double in size. Bake at 350 degrees for 30 minutes or until a deep golden brown. Makes 2 loaves.

Instructions for Hand Mixing

Dissolve yeast in ¼ cup lukewarm water. Combine remaining 2¾ cups water, oatmeal, molasses, and nonfat dry milk; add half the white flour and half the whole wheat flour, one cup at a time, beating

Lion House Raisin Bread and Whole Wheat Bread

well after each addition. Add yeast, remaining flour, shortening, and salt. Mix well; knead until dough is smooth and elastic. Place in covered bowl in warm place until double in size. Knead 1 minute to force out air bubbles. Mold into two loaves. Place in 2 well-greased loaf pans. Cover and let rise until double in size. Bake at 350 degrees for 30 minutes. Remove from pans to cool. Brush tops of loaves with butter.

Banana Nut Bread

6	large or 8 medium bananas, very ripe
4	eggs
2	cups sugar
¾	cup oil
4	cups flour
1	teaspoon baking soda
2	teaspoons salt
2	teaspoons baking powder
½	cup walnuts, chopped

Grease well and flour 2 large loaf pans; set aside. Peel bananas and place in large mixing bowl; mash bananas well. Add eggs, sugar, and oil; mix until well blended. In separate bowl, mix flour, baking soda, salt, and baking powder. Add to banana mixture. Mix until blended. Add nuts and mix briefly. (Overmixing causes tunnels and a coarse texture.) Pour into prepared pans. Bake at 325 degrees for 45 to 50 minutes or until wooden toothpick inserted in center comes out clean. Makes 2 loaves.

Note: Make smaller loaves if desired, baking for shorter amount of time.

Janell's Poppy Seed Bread

¼	cup butter, melted
3⅓	tablespoons oil
2	eggs
½	cup milk
¾	cup sugar
½	teaspoon vanilla
½	teaspoon almond extract
1	cup flour

½	teaspoon salt
1	teaspoon baking powder
¾	teaspoon poppy seeds
	Orange Almond Icing (below)

Grease and flour 8x4-inch loaf pan; set aside. In large mixing bowl, cream butter, oil, eggs, milk, sugar, vanilla, and almond extract. In separate bowl, mix flour, salt, baking powder, and poppy seeds. Add to first mixture and blend well, but do not overmix. (Overmixing causes tunnels and a coarse texture.) Pour into loaf pan and bake at 325 degrees for 45 minutes. Serve plain or ice with Orange Almond Icing. Makes 1 loaf.

Orange Almond Icing

1	tablespoon orange juice
¼	teaspoon vanilla
¼	teaspoon almond extract
¼	cup powdered sugar

In small bowl, mix all ingredients together.

Aloha Bread

1	cup butter
2	cups sugar
4	eggs
1	cup mashed bananas
4	cups flour
2	teaspoons baking powder
1	teaspoon baking soda
¾	teaspoon salt
1	can (20 ounces) crushed pineapple, drained
¾	cup chopped pecans
1	cup coconut

Grease 2 large 8x4-inch loaf pans; set aside. In large mixing bowl, cream butter and sugar. Add eggs; stir in bananas. In separate bowl, mix flour, baking powder, baking soda, and salt; add to banana mixture. Blend well, but do not overmix. (Overmixing causes tunnels and a coarse texture.) Add pineapple, pecans, and coconut; mix on low speed until blended. Pour into prepared pans. (Pans should be two-thirds full.) Bake at 325 degrees for 60 to 80 minutes. Makes 2 large loaves.

Cherry Nut Bread

1	cup sugar
½	cup oil
2	eggs
1	teaspoon vanilla
2¼	cups flour
1	teaspoon baking powder
1	jar (8 ounces) maraschino cherries, drained (reserve juice), and slightly chopped
½	cup walnuts, chopped

Grease and flour two 8x4-inch loaf pans or line with waxed paper; set aside. In large mixing bowl, cream sugar and oil; add eggs and beat well. Stir in vanilla. In separate bowl, mix flour and baking powder. Measure ½ cup maraschino cherry juice, or add water to juice to make ½ cup. Alternately add flour mixture and maraschino cherry juice to creamed mixture until all ingredients are blended. Stir in cherries and nuts. Pour into loaf pans; bake at 325 degrees for 55 to 60 minutes or until wooden toothpick inserted in center comes out clean. Makes 2 loaves.

Date Nut Bread

1¼	cups flour
1⅓	teaspoons baking soda
¾	teaspoon salt
⅔	cup dates, chopped
⅔	cup boiling water
⅔	cup brown sugar, lightly packed
2½	tablespoons oil
2	eggs
⅓	cup nuts, chopped

Line 8x4-inch loaf pan with waxed paper; set aside. In medium bowl, mix flour, baking soda, and salt; set aside. Place chopped dates in small bowl. Pour boiling water over dates and allow to cool until lukewarm. While dates are cooling, cream brown sugar, oil, and eggs in large mixing bowl. Blend in date mixture. Add flour mixture, then chopped nuts. Mix well. Pour into loaf pan; bake at 325 degrees for 35 to 40 minutes. Makes 1 loaf, 10 to 12 slices.

Chocolate Zucchini Bread

2	ounces unsweetened chocolate (2 blocks), melted
2	cups zucchini, grated
2	cups flour, all purpose
1	teaspoon salt
1	teaspoon soda
½	teaspoon baking powder
½	teaspoon cinnamon
3	eggs
1	cup sugar
1	cup brown sugar
1	cup oil
1	teaspoon vanilla
1	cup chocolate chips, semi-sweet

Prepare two 8x4-inch loaf pans by greasing and flouring or by lining with parchment paper. Melt unsweetened chocolate and set aside. Wash and grate zucchini; set aside. Measure flour, salt, soda, baking powder, and cinnamon into a bowl, stir, and set aside. Place eggs in mixing bowl and beat. Add the sugars, oil, melted chocolate, and vanilla; beat until creamy. Add the zucchini and stir together. Mix in dry ingredients until incorporated. Add the chocolate chips and mix in. Bake at 325 degrees for 45 to 50 minutes. Makes 2 loaves.

Lion House Pumpkin Bread

1⅓	cups vegetable oil
5	eggs
1	can (16 ounces) pumpkin
2	cups flour
2	cups sugar
1	teaspoon salt
1	teaspoon cinnamon
1	teaspoon nutmeg
1	teaspoon baking soda
2	packages (3 ounces each) instant vanilla pudding mix
1	cup chopped nuts

Grease well 2 large 8x4-inch loaf pans; set aside. Mix oil, eggs, and pumpkin in mixing bowl; beat well. In separate bowl, sift together flour, sugar, salt, cinnamon, nutmeg, and baking soda. Add to pumpkin mixture and mix till blended. Stir in pudding mix and nuts. Pour into prepared loaf pans. Bake at 350 degrees for 1 hour. Makes 2 loaves.

Cherry Nut Bread, Janell's Poppy Seed Bread,
Chocolate Zucchini Bread

Cranberry Nut Bread

2 cups flour
1 teaspoon baking powder
½ teaspoon baking soda
1 teaspoon salt
⅓ cup butter
¾ cup sugar
2 eggs
¾ cup orange juice
1 tablespoon grated orange peel
1 cup fresh or frozen cranberries (chopped, if desired)
½ cup chopped nuts

Grease and flour large 8x4-inch loaf pan or two small 7x3-inch loaf pans; set aside. In medium bowl, mix flour, baking powder, baking soda, and salt. In mixer bowl, cream butter until soft; add sugar. Beat until creamy; add eggs, orange juice, and orange peel. Beat until well mixed. Scrape down sides and bottom of bowl; add dry ingredients. Mix at low speed until blended, but do not overmix. Stir in cranberries and nuts by hand. Pour batter into prepared loaf pan or pans. Bake at 350 degrees 45 to 50 minutes for large loaf, less time for small loaves. Cool completely before slicing. Makes 1 large or 2 small loaves.

Zucchini Bread

3 cups flour
1 teaspoon baking soda
½ teaspoon baking powder
2 teaspoons cinnamon
3 eggs
1 cup oil
2 cups sugar
1 tablespoon vanilla
2 cups zucchini, grated
1 cup walnuts, chopped

Grease well large 8x4-inch loaf pan or 2 small 7x3-inch loaf pans. Set aside. In large bowl, mix flour, baking soda, baking powder, and cinnamon. Set aside. In separate mixing bowl, beat eggs until light and foamy. Add oil, sugar, vanilla, and zucchini; mix well. Add flour mixture and mix just

until moist. (Overmixing causes tunnels and a coarse texture.) Fold in nuts. Pour into prepared pan or pans. (Pans should be about two-thirds full.) Bake at 325 degrees for 45 to 50 minutes for large loaf or 35 minutes for small loaves, or until wooden toothpick inserted in center comes out clean. Do not overbake. Serves 10 to 12.

Dilly Casserole Bread

1 package (1 tablespoon) dry yeast
¼ cup lukewarm water
1 cup creamed cottage cheese, heated to lukewarm
2 tablespoons sugar
1 tablespoon instant minced onion, or 2 tablespoons finely chopped fresh onion
1 tablespoon butter or margarine
1 tablespoon dill weed
1 teaspoon salt
¼ teaspoon baking soda
1 unbeaten egg
2¼ to 2½ cups flour

Soften yeast in water. In mixing bowl, combine cottage cheese, sugar, onion, butter, dill weed, salt, baking soda, egg, and softened yeast. Add flour to form stiff dough, beating well after each addition. Cover; let rise in warm place (85 to 90 degrees), until light and double in size, about 50 to 60 minutes. Stir dough down. Turn into well-greased, 8-inch round, 1½ to 2-quart casserole. Let rise in warm place until light, 30 to 40 minutes. Bake at 350 degrees for 40 to 50 minutes, until golden brown. Brush with soft butter and sprinkle with salt. Makes 1 round loaf.

Buttermilk Scones

1 quart buttermilk
2 packages (2 tablespoons) dry yeast
¼ cup lukewarm water
¼ cup sugar
2 eggs, beaten
2 tablespoons oil
1½ teaspoons salt

3 teaspoons baking powder
½ teaspoon baking soda
8 cups flour
   Cooking oil or shortening for frying

Heat buttermilk until warm. Soften yeast in luke-warm water. In large bowl, combine buttermilk, sugar, eggs, oil, salt, baking powder, baking soda, and 4 cups flour. Add yeast; beat until smooth. Add remaining flour to make soft dough. Allow to rise, covered, until double in size. Punch down and place in refrigerator overnight.

When ready to fry, heat oil or shortening to 375 degrees. Roll dough out on floured board. Cut into squares about 2x2 inches. Stretch each piece a little and drop into hot fat. Fry on one side until golden; turn and fry on other side. Drain on paper towels. Serve hot with honey butter. Makes about 60 to 100 scones, depending on size. Dough will keep in refrigerator 3 to 4 days. Punch down from time to time and cover tightly with foil or damp cloth.

Honey Butter

½ cup butter
¼ teaspoon vanilla
½ cup honey

Whip softened butter. Add vanilla and honey gradually. Beat for 20 minutes. Makes 1 cup.

The Inn at Temple Square's Raspberry Honey Butter

1 pound butter, unsalted
8 ounces honey
8 ounces raspberry preserves
1 teaspoon vanilla

Whip butter until light and fluffy. Add honey, raspberry preserves, and vanilla. Continue to whip until mixed.

Refrigerator Bran Muffins

2 cups boiling water
4 cups bran cereal (Bran Buds® or All Bran®)
1 pound dates, pitted and chopped, or 2 cups raisins (less if using Raisin Bran®)
5 cups flour (part whole wheat flour, if desired)
1 teaspoon salt
5 teaspoons baking soda
1 cup salad oil
2 cups sugar
4 eggs, beaten
1 quart buttermilk
2 cups bran flakes cereal or Raisin Bran®

Pour boiling water over bran cereal and dates. Sift dry ingredients together. Cream oil and sugar; add eggs, hot bran mixture, dry ingredients, and buttermilk. Add the 2 cups bran flakes cereal. Mix just enough to combine. Bake in greased and floured muffin tins or line with cupcake papers at 400 degrees for 15 to 20 minutes. Makes 6 dozen muffins. Batter may be stored in covered container in refrigerator up to 6 weeks. Bake any amount as desired.

Lion House Fruit Muffins

⅔ cup sugar
⅓ cup shortening
1 egg
¼ cup honey
1 cup milk
2 cups flour
1 teaspoon baking soda
1 teaspoon baking powder
1 teaspoon salt
½ cup drained canned fruit, cut in small pieces

Cream sugar and shortening; add egg and mix well. Add honey and milk, scraping bowl often. Add sifted dry ingredients and mix at low speed just until blended. Fold in drained fruit. Fill greased muffin tins ¾ full. Bake at 375 degrees for 20 minutes. Makes 1 dozen muffins.

Refrigerator Rolls

¼ cup butter or margarine
¼ cup sugar
1 cup milk, scalded
1 package (1 tablespoon) dry yeast
1 tablespoon sugar
¼ cup lukewarm water
2 teaspoons salt
4 cups flour
3 eggs

Add butter and ¼ cup sugar to hot milk; cool. Combine yeast, 1 tablespoon sugar, and lukewarm water; let stand 5 minutes to soften yeast. Add salt to flour. Combine milk and yeast mixtures, and add 1 cup flour gradually, beating until smooth after each addition. (This makes a soft dough, and most or all of the flour can be handled by electric mixer.)

Cover bowl and place out of draft until dough rises to about triple in size. Punch down. Cover again and place in refrigerator overnight, or until thoroughly chilled (dough will keep well up to 5 days). When ready to use, remove from refrigerator; roll and shape rolls while cold. (Soft dough is easier to handle when chilled.) Place rolls on greased pans; brush with melted butter. Let rolls rise 1 to 1½ hours. Bake at 375 degrees for 10 to 15 minutes, or until desired doneness.

Note: This dough may be left to rise for 5 to 6 hours without doing any harm. A good recipe for occasions when it is uncertain how long rolls will need to wait before baking.

The Inn at Temple Square's Dinner Rolls with Orange Glaze

2½ tablespoons dry yeast
2 cups warm water (110 degrees)
⅓ cup sugar
¼ cup butter, softened
1 tablespoon salt
½ cup dry milk powder
4½ cups flour
1 egg
The Inn at Temple Square's Orange Roll Glaze (below)

In large bowl of electric mixer, combine yeast and water; let stand 5 minutes. Add sugar, butter, salt, dry milk, 2 cups flour, and egg; beat until very smooth. Mix in 2 more cups flour, one at a time, until smooth. Mix in ½ cup of flour, (by mixer, if not too stiff, or by hand) until well-mixed. Turn dough onto lightly floured board and knead until dough is smooth and satiny. Gather dough into a ball and place in greased bowl. Let rise in warm place until double in size. Turn dough onto lightly floured board. Roll out and cut or mold rolls into desired shapes. Place on greased baking sheets or pans. Brush rolls with melted butter; let rise in warm place about 1½ hours. Bake at 400 degrees for 15 to 20 minutes, or until desired brownness. Allow to cool, and ice with orange roll glaze. Makes about 2 dozen rolls.

Note: The entire mixing process may be done by hand, taking care to beat and knead dough thoroughly to develop gluten in dough. Soft dough makes lighter, more tender rolls. Always add flour gradually and keep dough as soft as you can handle it. Refrigerate dough after mixing, at least 1 hour or overnight, for easier handling. Remove dough from refrigerator about 3 hours before baking.

The Inn at Temple Square's Orange Roll Glaze

Orange peel from ½ orange, grated fine
Juice from ½ orange
2 cups powdered sugar

Mix zest, orange juice, and powered sugar until smooth. Spread on rolls while still slightly warm.

Carrot Cake

- 2 cups flour
- 1 teaspoon salt
- 1 teaspoon baking soda
- 2 teaspoons cinnamon
- ½ cup coconut, ground
- ½ cup walnuts, ground
- ½ cup raisins, ground
- 3 cups carrots, peeled and grated
- 2 cups sugar
- 1 cup oil
- 4 eggs
- Cream Cheese Icing (below)

Lightly grease and flour (or spray with nonstick cooking spray and line the bottom with parchment paper or wax paper) two 9-inch round or square cake pans or a 9x13-inch pan.

Measure dry ingredients into bowl and stir until well mixed. In separate bowl, mix coconut, walnuts, and raisins. Grind this mixture in food processor or blender until very fine (or chop with knife until very, very fine). Peel and grate carrots. Combine sugar and oil and mix well. Add eggs and beat until creamy. Add dry ingredients and beat until well blended. Add nut mixture and carrots and beat until blended. Divide equally into pans and bake at 350 degrees for 40 to 45 minutes. Allow to cool 10 minutes before removing from pans and placing on cooling racks. When completely cool, frost with cream cheese icing.

Cream Cheese Icing

- 2 packages (8 ounces each) cream cheese, softened
- ½ cup butter, at room temperature
- 5 cups powdered sugar
- 2 teaspoon vanilla

Beat cream cheese until softened. Add butter and mix until blended. Add 3 cups powdered sugar and beat until blended. Add remaining powdered sugar and vanilla and beat until smooth and fluffy. Do not overmix this or icing will be runny.

Oatmeal Cake

- 1½ cups boiling water
- 1 cup rolled oats
- ½ cup shortening
- 1 cup brown sugar
- 1 cup sugar
- 2 eggs, well beaten
- 1½ cups flour
- 1 teaspoon cinnamon
- ½ teaspoon nutmeg
- 1 teaspoon baking soda
- ½ teaspoon salt
- Topping (below)

Pour boiling water over oats and let stand until cool. Cream shortening with sugars and eggs until fluffy. Add oats and water mixture. Sift flour with other dry ingredients and blend into creamed mixture. Pour into greased and lightly floured 9x13-inch baking pan. Bake at 350 degrees for 35 to 45 minutes or until cake tests done. Immediately spread topping on baked cake.

Topping

- ½ cup butter or margarine
- 1 cup brown sugar
- ⅓ cup evaporated milk
- 1 cup coconut
- 1 cup nuts, chopped
- 1 teaspoon vanilla

Melt butter; blend in sugar. Add remaining ingredients and spread on baked hot cake. Place under broiler for 1 to 2 minutes.

Sting of the Bee (Bienenstich) Cake

Prepare Topping and allow to cool while preparing Cake.

Topping

½ cup butter (no substitutes)
½ cup sugar
2 tablespoons milk
1 cup almonds, slivered
2 teaspoons vanilla

In medium saucepan, melt butter until almost boiling. Add sugar and bring to a boil, stirring constantly. Slowly add milk; stir carefully as mixture will pop. Return to a boil and add almonds. Bring to a boil once again. Remove from heat and stir in vanilla. Allow to cool to room temperature if made early in the day; or cool in refrigerator until thick and cool to the touch. For best product, topping should be same temperature as dough.

Cake

1 cup butter (no substitutes)
⅔ cup sugar
2 eggs
3 cups flour, sifted
1 tablespoon baking powder
1 teaspoon salt
½ cup milk
Butter Cream Filling (below)

With mixer, cream butter and sugar until soft; add eggs and mix well. Mix in dry ingredients; slowly add milk. Beat until dough is thick and does not stick when touched.

Prepare 10-inch springform pan: Place parchment or waxed paper on bottom of pan. Attach side of pan; spray side with nonstick cooking spray and lightly dust with flour.

Press dough evenly in springform pan. Sprinkle small amount of flour on top of dough; gently tap dough down with flat bottom of a cup. (Dough should feel firm and press against the sides of pan.) Pour topping on dough and spread evenly.

Cover pan with foil and bake at 375 degrees for 30 minutes. Remove foil and bake for an additional 10 to 15 minutes, until cake looks firm and golden brown. Allow to cool. Split in half horizontally, fill with Butter Cream Filling and raspberry preserves.

Note: This cake is similar to biscuits in texture.

Butter Cream Filling

1 cup butter (no substitutes)
2 cups powdered sugar
2 egg yolks
2 teaspoons vanilla
½ cup raspberry preserves

Soften butter. Beat in powdered sugar, egg yolks, and vanilla until fluffy. Spread on bottom of split cake. Spread preserves on top of butter cream and replace cake top.

Whipped Cream Valentine Cake

1 10-inch angel food cake, baked and cooled
1 package (10 ounces) frozen strawberries or raspberries, thawed
1 envelope (1 tablespoon) unflavored gelatin
2 cups heavy cream, whipped until stiff
4 tablespoons sugar
1 teaspoon vanilla

Cut angel food cake into three horizontal layers. Drain juice from thawed strawberries or raspberries into small bowl. Sprinkle gelatin over juice and allow to stand until softened. Set small bowl in larger bowl of hot water and stir until gelatin dissolves. Combine gelatin mixture with berries and cool slightly. (If mixture cools too much, gelatin will set.) Add sugar and vanilla to whipped cream. Fold berries into cream. (Fruit that may seem too juicy will soon set up.) Alternate cake layers with generous layers of cream mixture. Adjust top cake layer and spread remaining cream over entire top and sides of cake. Refrigerate until firm. Makes 10 to 12 servings.

Sting of the Bee Cake

German's Sweet Chocolate Cake

1   package (4 ounces) German's sweet chocolate
½   cup boiling water
¾   cup shortening, butter, or margarine*
1¾   cups sugar
4   eggs
1   teaspoon vanilla
2¾   cups sifted cake flour
1   teaspoon baking soda
1   teaspoon salt
1   cup buttermilk*
    Coconut Pecan Frosting (below)

Melt chocolate in ½ cup boiling water; cool. Cream butter; gradually add sugar, creaming until light and fluffy. Add eggs, one at a time, beating well after each addition. Blend in vanilla and melted chocolate. Sift flour with baking soda and salt. Alternately add flour mixture and buttermilk to chocolate mixture, beating after each addition until smooth. Line bottoms of three 9-inch layer pans with paper. Pour cake batter into pans. Bake at 375 degrees for 30 to 35 minutes, or until toothpick inserted in center of each layer comes out clean. Cool cake in pans 10 minutes. Remove from pans and finish cooling on racks. Peel off paper. Spread Coconut Pecan Frosting between layers and over top of cake.

Note: For altitudes below 3,000 feet, use 2 cups sugar. For altitudes 5,000 to 7,000 feet, use 1½ cups sugar.

* If using vegetable shortening, use 1 cup plus 2 tablespoons buttermilk.

Coconut Pecan Frosting

3   egg yolks
1   cup sugar
1   cup evaporated milk
½   cup butter or margarine
1   teaspoon vanilla
1⅓   cups flaked coconut
1   cup chopped pecans

Combine egg yolks, sugar, milk, butter, and vanilla. Cook and stir over medium heat until thickened, 12 to 15 minutes. Add coconut and pecans. Beat until thick enough to spread. Makes 3 cups, enough to cover tops of three 8- or 9-inch layers or one 9x13-inch cake.

Chocolate Sheet Cake

½   cup butter or margarine, softened
½   cup shortening, softened
4   tablespoons cocoa
1   cup water
2   cups flour
2   cups sugar
½   cup buttermilk
1   teaspoon baking soda
1   teaspoon cinnamon
1   teaspoon vanilla
2   eggs, beaten
    Dash salt
    Frosting (below)

Mix butter, shortening, cocoa, and water; bring to boil. Sift together flour and sugar. Pour butter mixture over flour and sugar; mix well. Add buttermilk, baking soda, cinnamon, vanilla, eggs, and salt; mix well. Bake at 400 degrees for 20 minutes in greased and floured jelly roll pan (10x15-inch). Five minutes before cake is done, prepare frosting.

Frosting

½   cup butter or margarine
4   tablespoons cocoa
1   teaspoon vanilla
6   tablespoons milk
4   cups powdered sugar
1   cup chopped nuts

Melt butter; add cocoa, vanilla, and milk, and bring to boil. Remove from heat and add powdered sugar and nuts. Mix well. Frost cake while hot.

Black Devil's Food Cake

⅓   cup shortening
1½   cups sugar
3   eggs, well beaten

German's Sweet Chocolate Cake

⅔ cup cocoa
½ cup hot water
2 cups flour
½ teaspoon salt
1 teaspoon baking soda
1 cup thick sour cream
1 teaspoon vanilla

Cream well shortening and sugar; add eggs. Beat cocoa in hot water until smooth; add to creamed mixture. Sift dry ingredients together; add to sugar mixture alternately with sour cream. Add vanilla and beat well. Bake in three 8-inch or two 9-inch greased and floured layer pans, at 350 degrees for 20 to 30 minutes or until cake tests done. Remove cake from oven to wire racks. Let cool 10 minutes. Turn from pans and cool on wire rack. Frost with desired frosting.

Chocolate Cream Cake

Chocolate Cream Cake

1   package devil's food cake mix
    Chocolate Frosting (below)
    Stabilized Whipping Cream (below)

Following package directions, prepare and bake cake mix in two 9-inch round layers. Cool and split layers horizontally. (Only three of the four layers are used in this recipe. Freeze extra layer for later use.) While cake is baking, prepare Chocolate Frosting and Stabilized Whipping Cream.

To assemble cake: Place one layer of cake on serving plate. Spread evenly with half the Stabilized Whipping Cream, to within half an inch of edge of cake. Place another cake layer on top of cream; then another layer of cream. Alternate cake and cream for a total of five layers, ending with cake layer. Gently press down on top layer to set layers together. Frost entire cake with Chocolate Frosting. Garnish with a few chopped walnuts.

Chocolate Frosting

4   tablespoons cocoa
3   cups powdered sugar
4   tablespoons butter or margarine,
      softened
2 to 3   tablespoons milk
1   teaspoon vanilla

In mixing bowl, mix cocoa and powdered sugar. Add softened butter, milk, and vanilla. Beat until smooth.

Stabilized Whipping Cream

1   envelope (1 tablespoon) unflavored
      gelatin
¼   cup cold water
3   cups heavy whipping cream
¾   cup powdered sugar
1½   teaspoons vanilla

In small saucepan, combine gelatin with water; let stand until thick. Stir constantly over low heat until just dissolved. Remove from heat and allow to cool slightly but do not allow to thicken. In large mixing bowl, whip cream, sugar, and vanilla until slightly thick. On low speed, gradually add gelatin, then beat on high until cream is thick.

Note: Stabilized Whipping Cream will hold up for 4 to 5 days without separating. It may also be used to garnish cheesecakes or in any recipe calling for whipped cream or nondairy whipped topping.

Whole Wheat Crumb Cake

1½   cups whole wheat flour
¾   cup granulated sugar
¾   cup brown sugar
½   cup shortening
¾   cup dates, chopped
¾   cup walnuts, chopped
½   teaspoon salt
¼   teaspoon nutmeg
2   eggs
¾   cup milk
1   teaspoon vanilla
1   teaspoon baking soda
    Topping (below)

Mix flour, sugars, shortening, dates, walnuts, salt, and nutmeg by hand until well blended (do not use electric mixer). In separate bowl, beat eggs; add milk, vanilla, and baking soda. Add liquid ingredients to dry ingredients. Stir just until dry ingredients are moistened. Pour into well-greased 9x13-inch pan. Sprinkle Topping over batter. Bake at 350 degrees for 25 minutes. Serve warm, with or without whipped cream or ice cream, or caramel, lemon, or vanilla sauce.

Topping

½   cup white sugar
½   cup brown sugar
½   cup chopped nuts

With fingers, mix sugars and chopped nuts together until blended.

Coconut Brunch Cake

- 4 eggs
- 2 cups sugar
- 1 cup salad oil
- 3 cups flour
- ½ teaspoon baking soda
- ½ teaspoon baking powder
- ½ teaspoon salt
- 1 cup buttermilk
- 2 teaspoons coconut flavoring
- 1 cup coconut
- 1 cup walnuts, chopped
- 1 cup sugar
- ½ cup water
- 3 tablespoons butter or margarine

In large mixing bowl, beat eggs, sugar, and salad oil. In separate bowl, sift flour, baking soda, baking powder, and salt. Add dry ingredients to creamed mixture alternately with buttermilk. Add coconut flavoring, coconut, and walnuts. Generously grease and flour a 10-inch Bundt pan. Pour batter into pan. Bake at 350 degrees for 1 hour.

In the meantime, in saucepan mix 1 cup sugar, water, and butter or margarine. Bring to boil and cook for 5 minutes. When cake is done, pour hot syrup over top of cake. Allow to stand for 4 hours, then remove from pan.

Angel Food Cake

- 1 cup plus 2 tablespoons sifted cake flour
- 1½ cups sifted sugar
- 1¾ cups (10 to 12) egg whites, at room temperature
- ¼ teaspoon salt
- 1¼ teaspoons cream of tartar
- 1 teaspoon vanilla
- ¼ teaspoon almond extract

Sift together flour and ½ cup sugar. In large bowl, combine egg whites, salt, cream of tartar, and flavorings. Beat with flat wire whip, sturdy egg beater, or at high speed of electric mixer until soft peaks form. Add remaining 1 cup sugar gradually, ¼ cup at a time, beating well after each addition. (If beating by hand, beat 25 strokes after each addition.) Sift in flour mixture, one-fourth at a time, folding in with 15 fold-over strokes each time, turning bowl frequently. Do not stir or beat. After last addition, use 10 to 20 extra folding strokes.

Pour batter into ungreased 9- or 10-inch tube pan. Bake at 375 degrees for 35 to 40 minutes for 9-inch cake or 30 to 35 minutes for 10-inch cake, or until cake springs back when pressed lightly. Cool cake in pan, upside down, 1 to 2 hours. Then loosen from sides and center tube with knife and gently pull out cake. An angel cake pan with a removable bottom is ideal for removing cake in perfect condition.

Poppy Seed Cake

- 1 package (18 ounces) yellow cake mix
- 1 package (3¾ ounces) instant vanilla pudding mix
- 4 eggs
- 1 cup thick sour cream
- ½ cup water
- 1 teaspoon rum flavoring
- ½ cup butter or margarine, melted
- ¼ cup poppy seeds

In large bowl of electric mixer, combine cake and pudding mixes, eggs, sour cream, water, rum flavoring, butter, and poppy seeds. Blend well on low speed, then beat at medium speed for 5 minutes. Pour batter into well-greased and lightly floured Bundt pan. Bake at 350 degrees for about 45 minutes, or until cake tests done. Remove from oven and cool in pan for 15 minutes. Turn out onto cake rack and cool completely. Sift a light dusting of powdered sugar over cake, if desired.

Note: This delicious cake dessert may also be sliced thin and served as a bread with fruit salad.

Chiffon Cake

1¼ cups sugar
1 tablespoon baking powder
2¼ cups cake flour
1 teaspoon salt
½ cup salad oil
5 egg yolks
¾ cup water
2 teaspoons vanilla
1 cup (7 to 8 large) egg whites
½ teaspoon cream of tartar

In mixing bowl, sift dry ingredients together. Add oil, egg yolks, water, and vanilla; beat until smooth. Beat egg whites with cream of tartar until stiff. Pour yolk mixture over whipped whites, folding together until blended. Bake in ungreased 10-inch tube pan at 325 degrees for 55 minutes. When cake tests done, invert tube pan and let hang until cool.

Lemon Chiffon Cake Frosting

2 cans lemon pie filling
1 carton (8 ounces) Cool Whip®

Cut chiffon cake horizontally into 3 layers. Separate layers. Spread a thin layer of lemon pie filling on cut side of bottom layer, then place the next layer on top of the pie filling and spread the top of that layer with pie filling. (It should take about ½ can for each layer.) Fold ¾ can of pie filling into the Cool Whip and frost inside the hole, ouside the cake, and on top of the cake. Cut, and enjoy! This cake must be kept in the refrigerator.

Chiffon Cake

Orange Sponge Cake

8 eggs, separated
¼ teaspoon salt
1 teaspoon cream of tartar
1⅔ cups sugar
   Grated rind from one orange
⅓ cup orange juice
1 cup plus 2 tablespoons flour, sifted
½ cup almonds, blanched and toasted
1 cup cream, whipped

Beat egg whites and salt until foamy; add cream of tartar and beat until soft peaks form. Gradually add 1 cup sugar, beating until stiff but not dry; set aside. In separate bowl, beat egg yolks until thick and lemon-colored. Add remaining ⅔ cup sugar, orange rind and juice; beat well. Add flour; mix well. Gently fold egg whites into batter. Pour batter into ungreased 10-inch tube pan. Bake at 325 degrees for 1 hour. Remove from oven and invert for 1 hour. Coarsely chop almonds. Spread whipped cream on cake and sprinkle with almonds, or glaze with Orange Butter Glaze or Lemon Butter Glaze (below).

Orange Butter Glaze

1½ tablespoons milk
1 tablespoon butter
1¼ cups powdered sugar
1 tablespoon orange juice
½ teaspoon grated orange rind

Heat milk and butter together. Stir in sugar and mix until smooth. Add orange juice and rind; beat until shiny. Add a drop or two more liquid if needed to make desired spreading consistency. Makes about ½ cup, or enough to glaze top of 10-inch tube cake, or 8- or 9-inch square cake, or 9x5-inch loaf.

Lemon Butter Glaze

Prepare as for Orange Butter Glaze, substituting lemon juice and rind for orange juice and rind.

Peppermint Angel Food Dessert

¾ cup crushed red and white peppermint stick candy
½ cup milk
½ envelope (1½ teaspoons) unflavored gelatin
2 teaspoons water
1 pint whipped cream, whipped until stiff
1 angel food cake, sliced into 3 horizontal layers
½ cup chocolate syrup

Combine candy with milk; heat and stir until dissolved. Soften gelatin in water and add to milk and candy mixture. Chill until mixture starts to set; fold into whipped cream. Spread cream mixture over bottom layer of cake. Drizzle chocolate syrup over whipped cream mixture. Place another layer of cake on top and repeat layer of whipped cream and chocolate syrup. Repeat with third layer. Cover outside of cake with whipped cream mixture. Chill and serve. Makes 12 servings.

Strawberry Delight

1 package (3 ounces) strawberry gelatin
1 package (10 ounces) sliced frozen strawberries
1 tablespoon sugar
   Dash salt
1 cup whipped cream, whipped with 1 tablespoon sugar
½ of large angel food cake, torn in pieces

Dissolve gelatin in 1¼ cups boiling water. Stir in strawberries, sugar, and salt. Cool until gelatin is thick and syrupy. Fold in whipped cream, reserving about ¼ cup for garnish. Place half the cake pieces into 2- or 3-quart serving bowl. Pour half the strawberry cream mixture over cake. Add another layer of torn cake pieces and then remaining strawberry cream mixture. Refrigerate 1 to 2 hours or until set. Top each serving with dollop of whipped cream. Makes about 10 servings.

Angel Fluff

1   9-ounce loaf angel food cake
1   cup whipped cream, whipped until stiff
1   cup half-and-half cream
1   cup sugar
⅓   cup lemon juice
     Pineapple Sauce (below)

In large, attractive, 2-quart serving bowl, break cake into bite-sized pieces. In small bowl of electric mixer or with hand electric mixer, gradually whip half-and-half into a fluffy, thick liquid. Beat sugar gradually into cream mixture, then slowly beat in lemon juice. Pour mixture over cake pieces. Chill for at least 2 hours. Spoon onto dessert plates and serve with Pineapple Sauce. Makes 8 servings.

Pineapple Sauce

4   tablespoons cornstarch
1   cup sugar
2¼   cups pineapple juice
¼   cup lemon juice

In small saucepan, combine cornstarch and sugar; mix well. Add pineapple juice; cook on medium heat, stirring constantly, until clear and thickened, about 5 minutes. Add lemon juice. Remove from heat. Chill.

Gingerbread

½   cup sugar
½   cup butter or margarine
1   egg, well beaten
1   cup molasses
½   teaspoon salt
2½   cups sifted flour
1½   teaspoons baking soda
1   teaspoon cinnamon
1   teaspoon ginger
½   teaspoon powdered cloves
1   cup very hot water
     Bananas
     Whipped cream

Cream sugar and butter well. Add eggs and molasses; beat well. Sift dry ingredients together and add to creamed mixture. Add hot water and

beat until smooth (batter will be very thin). Pour into well-greased 9x13-inch baking pan. Bake at 350 degrees for about 40 minutes or until cake tests done. Serve warm or cold with sliced bananas and whipped cream.

Baker's Variation

Drain one 27-ounce can of pears. Place cut side of pear down in baking pan. Pour batter on top and bake as directed.

Caramel Pudding Cake

4   cups water
2   cups brown sugar
½   cup butter or margarine
1   cup sugar
1   cup chopped peeled apples
2   cups flour
1   teaspoon nutmeg
1   teaspoon cinnamon
2½   teaspoons baking powder
½   teaspoon salt
1½   teaspoons baking soda
1   cup milk
1   teaspoon vanilla
½   cup raisins
½   cup chopped nuts
     Whipped topping (optional)

Mix and boil together water, brown sugar, and ¼ cup butter or margarine; set aside. Cream remaining ¼ cup butter; add sugar. Cream thoroughly; add chopped apples. Sift dry ingredients together and add alternately with milk. Stir in remaining ingredients. Spread batter in greased 9x13-inch pan. Pour hot brown sugar and butter mixture over batter. Bake at 375 degrees for 45 minutes. Cut in squares and serve, warm or cold, with whipped topping, if desired. Makes 20 to 24 servings.

Cheesecake

Crust

- 1½ cups graham cracker crumbs, rolled fine
- 3 tablespoons sugar
- 6 tablespoons butter or margarine

Thoroughly mix ingredients. Press firmly onto bottom and sides of a 9- or 10-inch pie pan; set aside. Make filling.

Filling

- 3 packages (8 ounces each) softened cream cheese
- 1 cup sugar
- 3 eggs
- ¾ teaspoon vanilla
- 2 teaspoons lemon juice

Beat cream cheese well; add sugar a little at a time. Add eggs one at a time, then vanilla. Combine thoroughly. Pour into crust; fill to within half an inch of top to allow room for topping. Bake at 300 degrees for 55 to 60 minutes.

Topping

- 1 pint sour cream
- 3 tablespoons sugar
- ½ teaspoon vanilla

Whip sour cream. Add sugar gradually, then vanilla. Pour over cake and bake at 300 degrees for 10 minutes. Cool completely. Refrigerate until ready to serve. Top with desired fruit topping.

Lemon Cheesecake

- 1½ cups graham cracker crumbs, rolled fine
- 3 tablespoons butter or margarine, melted
- 3 packages (8 ounces each) cream cheese, softened
- 1 cup sugar
- 3 eggs
- ¾ teaspoon vanilla
- ⅓ cup lemon juice
- 1 pint sour cream
- 3 tablespoons sugar
- ½ teaspoon vanilla

Mix graham cracker crumbs and butter or margarine. Press firmly onto bottom and sides of 9- or 10-inch springform pan. In large mixer bowl, whip cream cheese; gradually add sugar; then add eggs one at a time. Stir in vanilla. Stir in lemon juice. Pour filling into crust. Bake at 300 degrees for 55 minutes. Whip sour cream; add sugar and vanilla. Spread on top of cheesecake and return to oven. Bake 10 more minutes. Cool before removing sides from springform pan. Garnish with lemon zest. Refrigerate until ready to serve. Makes 10 to 12 servings.

Pumpkin Cheesecake

- 1½ cups graham cracker crumbs, rolled fine
- 3 tablespoons butter or margarine, melted
- 3 packages (8 ounces each) cream cheese, softened
- 1 cup sugar
- 3 eggs
- ¾ teaspoon vanilla
- 1⅓ cups plus 2 tablespoons pumpkin
- ¾ teaspoon cinnamon
- ¼ teaspoon nutmeg
- ¼ teaspoon ginger
- ¼ teaspoon cloves
- ½ teaspoon salt
- 1 pint sour cream
- 3 tablespoons sugar
- ½ teaspoon vanilla

Mix graham cracker crumbs and butter or margarine. Press firmly onto bottom and sides of 9- or 10-inch springform pan. Whip cream cheese in mixer bowl; gradually add sugar, then eggs one at a time. Stir in vanilla. In separate bowl, combine pumpkin, cinnamon, nutmeg, ginger, cloves, and salt. Mix well; add to cream cheese mixture. Pour filling into crust. Bake at 300 degrees for 55 minutes. Whip sour cream; add sugar and vanilla. Spread on top of cheesecake and return to oven. Bake 10 more minutes. Cool before removing sides from springform pan. Garnish with a sprinkle of nutmeg. Refrigerate until ready to serve. Makes 10 to 12 servings.

Peppermint Cheesecake

- 2 cups Oreo® cookie crumbs, rolled fine
- 3 packages (8 ounces each) cream cheese, softened
- 1 cup sugar
- 3 eggs
- ¾ teaspoon vanilla
- 1 teaspoon peppermint extract
- 2 drops red food coloring
- 1 pint sour cream
- 3 tablespoons sugar
- ½ teaspoon vanilla
- Peppermint candy, crushed

Crush whole Oreo cookies, including frosting centers, to make 2 cups fine crumbs. Press evenly onto bottom and sides of 10-inch springform pan. Whip cream cheese in mixer bowl; gradually add sugar, then eggs one at a time. Stir in vanilla, peppermint extract, and red food coloring. Pour filling into crust. Bake at 300 degrees for 55 minutes. Whip sour cream; add sugar and vanilla. Spread on top of cheesecake and return to oven. Bake 10 more minutes. Cool before removing sides from springform pan. Garnish with crushed peppermint candy. Refrigerate until ready to serve. Makes 10 to 12 servings.

Chocolate Cheesecake

- 2 cups Oreo® cookie crumbs, rolled fine
- 3 packages (8 ounces each) cream cheese, softened
- 1 cup sugar
- 3 eggs
- ¾ teaspoon vanilla
- ⅓ cup chocolate syrup
- 1 pint sour cream
- 3 tablespoons sugar
- ½ teaspoon vanilla
- Chocolate chips

Crush whole Oreo cookies, including frosting centers, to make 2 cups fine crumbs. Press evenly onto bottom and sides of 10-inch springform pan. Whip cream cheese in mixer bowl; gradually add sugar, then eggs one at a time. Stir in vanilla. Stir in chocolate syrup. Pour filling into crust. Bake at 300 degrees for 55 minutes. Whip sour cream; add sugar and vanilla. Spread on top of cheesecake and return to oven. Bake 10 more minutes. Cool before removing sides from springform pan. Garnish with a few chocolate chips. Refrigerate until ready to serve. Makes 10 to 12 servings.

Easy Cherry Cheesecake

- 2 cups graham cracker crumbs
- ½ cup melted margarine or butter
- 1 package (8 ounces) softened cream cheese
- 2 tablespoons milk
- 1 cup powdered sugar
- ½ teaspoon vanilla
- 2 cups whipped topping (1 envelope topping mix prepared according to directions)
- 1 can cherry pie filling, or make your own from 1 can (16 ounces) pie cherries

In 9x13-inch pan, mix graham cracker crumbs with melted margarine. Level well with fork, then press firmly in bottom of pan. Combine cream cheese, milk, powdered sugar, and vanilla; mix until smooth. Fold in whipped topping. Spread over cracker crumbs. Cover with chilled cherry pie filling. Chill 2 hours. Makes 18 to 24 servings.

Picnic Brownies

Picnic Brownies

4	ounces baking chocolate
1	cup butter
2	cups sugar
2	teaspoons vanilla
1	teaspoon salt
4	eggs
1¾	cups flour
⅔	cup walnuts, pecans, or almonds, chopped
1	cup chocolate chips

Grease two 9-inch round pans. In top of double boiler or microwave-safe bowl, melt chocolate and butter. In medium bowl, mix sugar, vanilla, and salt; add to melted chocolate mixture and blend well. Add eggs, one at a time, beating well after each addition. Add flour and mix well. Divide batter equally into prepared pans. Spread evenly and sprinkle top of each with chopped nuts and chocolate chips. Bake at 350 degrees for 25 minutes. (Do not overbake.) Allow to cool completely before cutting. Run a thin knife between pan and brownies and turn upside down. You may need to shake hard to release brownies from pan. With knife that is longer than brownies are wide, cut brownies by pressing knife straight down through brownies; cut into 8 pie-shaped pieces. Makes 16 brownies.

Note: These brownies are named Picnic Brownies because they stack and travel very well.

Lemon Bars

½	cup soft butter or margarine
¼	cup powdered sugar
1	cup flour
2	eggs
1	cup sugar
2	tablespoons flour
2	tablespoons lemon juice
	Grated rind of ½ lemon

Cream butter and powdered sugar; add flour. Spread in 8x8-inch pan and bake at 325 degrees for 15 to 20 minutes. While crust is baking, prepare next layer: Beat eggs slightly; add sugar, flour, lemon juice, and rind. Mix well and pour over hot crust. Bake for an additional 18 to 25 minutes at 325 degrees. Remove from oven and sprinkle with sifted powdered sugar. Cool slightly before cutting into finger cookies. Good served with vanilla ice cream.

Note: This recipe may be doubled and baked in a 9x13-inch pan.

Oatmeal Fudge Bars

1	cup margarine
2	cups brown sugar
2	eggs
2	teaspoons vanilla
2½	cups flour
1	teaspoon baking soda
½	teaspoon salt
1½	cups quick-cooking oats
1	can (14 ounces) sweetened condensed milk
1	package (12 ounces) semisweet chocolate chips
¼	cup margarine
2	teaspoons vanilla
1	cup chopped walnuts (optional)

Grease a 9x13-inch baking pan; set aside. In large mixer bowl, cream margarine and brown sugar; add eggs and vanilla. In small bowl, sift flour, baking soda, and salt; add to creamed mixture. Mix in oats. In heavy saucepan, mix sweetened condensed milk, chocolate chips, and margarine; heat just till melted. Stir in vanilla and nuts. Spread two-thirds of dough into prepared baking pan. Spread with chocolate mixture. Drop remaining one-third of dough on top by spoonfuls. Bake at 350 degrees for 25 minutes. Cool, then cut into bars. Makes 36.

Old-Fashioned Sugar Cookies

Old-Fashioned Sugar Cookies

1½ cups sugar
⅔ cup butter or shortening (butter makes a better-tasting cookie)
2 eggs, beaten
2 tablespoons milk
1 teaspoon vanilla
3¼ cups flour
2½ teaspoons baking powder
½ teaspoon salt
    Decorative toppings (below)

Cream sugar and butter or shortening; add eggs, milk, and vanilla. Sift dry ingredients together and beat into creamed mixture, combining thoroughly. With hands, shape dough into a ball. Wrap and refrigerate 2 to 3 hours or overnight until dough is easy to handle.

Grease cookie sheets lightly. On lightly floured board, roll one-half or one-third of dough at a time, keeping remaining dough refrigerated. For crisp cookies, roll dough paper-thin. For softer cookies, roll ⅛-inch to ¼-inch thick. Cut into desired shapes with floured cookie cutter. Reroll trimmings and cut.

Place cookies half an inch apart on cookie sheets. Sprinkle with decorative toppings, if desired. Bake at 375 degrees about 8 minutes or until a very light brown. Remove cookies to racks to cool. Makes about 6 dozen cookies.

Decorative Toppings

Ice with Butter Cream Icing (below), or brush cookies with heavy cream or with a mixture of one egg white slightly beaten with one tablespoon water. Sprinkle with sugar, nonpareils, chopped nuts, shredded coconut, cut-up gumdrops, or butterscotch pieces.

Cutout Sugar Cookies

2	cups granulated sugar
1	cup shortening
3	eggs
1	cup milk
1	teaspoon vanilla
1	teaspoon lemon extract
6½	cups flour
1	teaspoon salt
1	teaspoon baking soda
3½	teaspoons baking powder
	Butter Cream Icing (below)

Line cookie sheet with waxed paper; set aside. In large mixer bowl, cream sugar, shortening, and eggs. Add milk, vanilla, and lemon extract; mix at low speed. In separate bowl, mix flour, salt, baking soda, and baking powder. Add to sugar mixture until well blended. Roll out ⅛-inch thick; cut into desired shapes. Bake at 400 degrees for 6 minutes, being careful not to overbake. Cookies should be light golden brown around the edges. Frost with Butter Cream Icing. Makes 5 to 6 dozen cookies.

Butter Cream Icing

¾	cup butter
¾	cup shortening
4⅔	cups powdered sugar

1½	teaspoons lemon juice
1½	teaspoons vanilla
⅓	cup water

In large mixer bowl, combine butter, shortening, and powdered sugar; beat until very creamy. Add lemon juice and vanilla; mix until well blended. Add water and mix until very light.

Chocolate Crackle Cookies

¼	cup shortening, melted
¼	cup cocoa
½	cup oil
2	cups sugar
4	eggs
2	teaspoons vanilla
2½	cups flour
½	teaspoon salt
1½	teaspoons baking powder
½	cup walnuts, chopped
½	cup chocolate chips (optional)
½ to 1	cup powdered sugar

Preheat oven to 350 degrees. In a large mixing bowl, cream together shortening, cocoa, oil, sugar, eggs, and vanilla until well mixed. Add flour, salt, and baking powder. Mix well, then add walnuts and chocolate chips, if desired. (Dough will be very sticky and almost runny.) Refrigerate dough for 2 to 3 hours or overnight. Drop and gently roll dough by tablespoonfuls in powdered sugar, being careful not to overhandle dough. Place on a greased or wax paper–covered cookie sheet. Bake for 9 to 10 minutes. Do not overbake. The cookie dough may be stored in the refrigerator for up to 5 days; baked cookies will store for at least 2 weeks, if well covered and refrigerated. These cookies freeze beautifully. Makes approximately 5 dozen cookies.

Iced Carrot Cookies

1	cup shortening
¾	cup sugar
2	eggs
1	cup cooked, mashed carrots
2	cups flour

2 teaspoons baking powder
½ teaspoon salt
¾ cup coconut
Orange Frosting (below)

In large mixing bowl, cream shortening and sugar. Add eggs; beat until fluffy. Add mashed carrots. Sift flour, baking powder, and salt; add to creamed mixture. Stir in coconut. Drop by teaspoonfuls onto greased cookie sheet. Bake at 400 degrees for 10 minutes. Cool, then ice with Orange Frosting (next page). Makes 4 dozen small cookies.

Orange Frosting

1 tablespoon orange juice
2 teaspoons grated orange peel
1 cup powdered sugar
2 tablespoons soft margarine

In small bowl, combine all ingredients; stir until well mixed.

Scotch Shortbread

2 cups (1 pound) butter, softened
1 cup sugar
4 cups flour

Cream butter and add sugar; beat until light and fluffy. Add flour and mix well. Chill several hours. Roll out about ¼-inch thick on floured board. Cut into 2x2-inch squares and place on ungreased baking sheet. Prick each cookie several times with fork. Bake at 325 degrees about 30 minutes, until cookies are delicately brown. Cool slightly before removing from cookie sheet. Makes about 40 cookies.

Old-Fashioned Filled Cookies

½ cup butter or margarine
¾ cup sugar
1 egg
2¼ cups flour
2 teaspoons baking powder
½ teaspoon salt
¼ teaspoon nutmeg

2 tablespoons milk
½ teaspoon vanilla
Raisin Filling (below)

Cream butter; add sugar and egg, and beat until fluffy. Sift flour, baking powder, salt, and nutmeg. Add to creamed mixture alternately with milk. Add vanilla. Chill dough 1 hour. Prepare Raisin Filling.

Roll dough ¼-inch thick. Cut with round cookie cutter about 3 inches in diameter. Cut 2 rounds for each cookie. Place about 1 teaspoon raisin filling in center of a round, and top with a second round. Press edges together with fingers or fork. Prick top with fork. Place on greased cookie sheet and bake at 350 degrees for 10 minutes or until just done.

Raisin Filling

1 cup ground raisins
¼ cup water
¼ cup sugar
¼ cup chopped nuts
1 teaspoon lemon juice

Place all ingredients in small saucepan and cook on low heat until thick, stirring constantly. Cool.

Layered Cookies

¼ pound butter or margarine
1 cup graham cracker crumbs
1 cup coconut
1 cup chocolate chips
1 cup butterscotch chips
1 cup nuts
1 can sweetened condensed milk

Melt butter in 9x13-inch pan. Sprinkle remaining ingredients over butter, in layers. Bake at 350 degrees for 30 minutes. Immediately after removing from oven, cut cookies away from sides of pan. Cut in squares while still warm.

Oatmeal Cookies

2 cups brown sugar
1 cup shortening
2 eggs

Peanut Butter Cookies, Chocolate Crackle Cookies, Snickerdoodles, Chocolate Chip Cookies

½   cup milk
2   cups quick rolled oats
½   teaspoon salt
1   teaspoon baking soda
1   teaspoon allspice
1   teaspoon cinnamon
1   teaspoon cloves
1   teaspoon nutmeg
2   cups flour
1   cup raisins
½   cup nuts

Cream sugar and shortening. Add eggs and milk; mix well. Add rolled oats. Sift together dry ingredients and mix in until smooth. Stir in raisins and nuts. Drop on cookie sheet and bake at 350 degrees for 10 minutes or until lightly browned. Makes 3 to 4 dozen cookies.

Chocolate Chip Cookies

1¾   cups softened butter
1¾   cups brown sugar
1¼   cups granulated sugar
4   eggs
5½   tablespoons water
1½   teaspoons vanilla
6   cups flour
1½   teaspoons salt
1½   teaspoons baking soda
3   cups chocolate chips

Line cookie sheet with waxed paper; set aside. In large mixing bowl, cream butter and sugars. Add eggs, water, and vanilla; mix until creamy. Add flour, salt, and baking soda; mix well. Gently fold in chocolate chips, mixing only until chips are evenly distributed. (Overmixing results in broken chips and discolored dough.) Drop by spoonfuls onto prepared cookie sheet. Bake at 350 degrees for 8 to 10 minutes or until golden brown. Makes 5 to 6 dozen 3½-inch cookies.

Peanut Butter Cookies

5¼   cups flour
2   teaspoons baking soda
1   teaspoon salt

1   cup butter
¾   cup shortening
1¾   cups sugar
1¾   cups brown sugar
4   eggs
1   teaspoon vanilla
¾   cup peanut butter

Line cookie sheet with waxed paper; set aside. In medium bowl, mix flour, baking soda, and salt; set aside. In large mixing bowl, cream butter, shortening, sugar, brown sugar, eggs, and vanilla. Stir in peanut butter. Add flour mixture and stir until well blended. Drop dough by tablespoonfuls onto cookie sheet. Using fork dipped in flour, flatten each cookie slightly in a crisscross pattern. Bake at 350 degrees for 8 to 10 minutes or until slightly golden around the edges. Do not overbake. Makes 5 dozen 3-inch cookies.

Snickerdoodles

½   cup granulated sugar
1¼   teaspoons cinnamon
1   cup butter, softened
2½   cups sugar
4   eggs
1   teaspoon vanilla
2½   tablespoons water
6   cups flour
2   teaspoons cream of tartar
1   teaspoon baking soda
½   teaspoon salt

In medium bowl, mix ½ cup sugar and cinnamon; set aside. In large mixing bowl, combine butter and 2½ cups sugar until light and fluffy. Add eggs, vanilla, and water; beat until fluffy. Add flour, cream of tartar, baking soda, and salt, turning mixer on and off in quick bursts at low speed until flour is nearly blended in. Continue mixing at medium speed until well mixed. Shape dough by rounded tablespoonfuls; roll in cinnamon-sugar mixture. Place on cookie sheet lined with waxed paper and bake at 350 degrees for 9 to 10 minutes or until golden brown. Makes 5 dozen 3-inch cookies.

Lion House Pie Dough

¼	cup butter
⅓	cup lard
¼	cup margarine
⅓	cup shortening
1	tablespoon sugar
½	teaspoon baking powder
1	teaspoon salt
1	tablespoon nonfat dry milk powder
1½	cups pastry flour plus 1½ cups bread flour, or 3 cups all-purpose flour
½	cup plus 1 tablespoon cold water

In mixer, cream butter, lard, margarine, and shortening. In bowl, mix sugar, baking powder, salt, and dry milk powder; add to creamed butter mixture and mix briefly. Add pastry flour and beat until blended. Add bread flour and mix slightly. Pour in water and beat again only until water is just blended in.

Divide dough into two or three balls. Roll each out on floured board. Line pie pan with dough and cut off excess dough. Flute edges. Prick holes in bottom with fork. Bake empty pie shell at 375 degrees for 12 to 15 minutes or until light golden brown. Or fill unbaked pie shell and bake according to recipe. Makes 2 to 3 pie shells.

Note: This crust may also be made by hand-cutting fats into dry ingredients.

Helpful Tips for Making Pies

For better sealing, brush edges of pie crusts with water just before putting top crust on.

For a beautiful golden top, brush pie crust with milk, cream, half-and-half, or evaporated milk, and sprinkle with sugar before baking.

Bake 4 to 8 pies at a time, and freeze in gallon Ziploc® bags. When pies are frozen, stack them on top of each other. When needed, take frozen pie out of plastic bag and bake at 325 degrees for 35 to 40 minutes.

Keep pie shells from shrinking by pricking bottoms with fork before baking. Then either bake shell on bottom of upside-down pie tin, or, after lining pie tin with dough, line with aluminum foil and pour beans, wheat, or rice in shell and bake for half the baking time. Lift out foil and contents and continue baking for remainder of baking time.

To Assemble All Fruit Pies

Spoon pie filling into unbaked 9-inch pie shell. Brush edge of dough with water and place top crust on pie. Seal crusts together by gently pressing around the edge of pie tin. Cut excess dough from edge of pie. Brush crust (but not edge) with milk, cream, half-and-half, or evaporated milk. Sprinkle sugar on top and bake at 375 degrees for 45 to 50 minutes or until golden brown. If crust cracks open or filling comes out the sides, pie is overdone.

Boysenberry Pie

	Pastry for 2-crust pie
1	bag (16 ounces) frozen boysenberries, thawed
1	cup sugar
¼	teaspoon salt
2½	tablespoons cornstarch

Pour thawed berries and juice into large mixing bowl. In separate bowl, mix sugar, salt, and cornstarch; pour on top of berries. Mix well with rubber spatula. Fill crust, add top crust, and bake at 375 degrees for 45 to 50 minutes or until golden brown. Makes 1 pie.

Quick Swiss Apple Pie

Apple Pie

Pastry for 2-crust pie
¾ to 1 cup sugar
2 tablespoons flour
½ to 1 teaspoon cinnamon
¼ to ½ teaspoon nutmeg
⅛ teaspoon salt
5 to 6 apples, peeled, cored, and sliced
2 tablespoons butter or margarine

Roll out bottom crust and line bottom and sides of pie tin. Roll out top crust, fold in half, and cut three ½-inch slits through both layers of crust; set aside. In separate bowl, combine dry ingredients and stir. Place sliced apples on top of dry ingredients; stir. Pour apple mixture in bottom of pie crust. Dot with small pieces of butter. Moisten edge of pie crust with water. Place top crust on pie and seal. Brush with milk, sprinkle with sugar, and bake at 375 degrees for 45 to 50 minutes or until apples test tender when sharp knife is inserted into vent hole on top of crust.

Note: The Lion House uses Golden Delicious apples, but any tart apple will make a wonderful pie.

A 30-ounce can of apple pie filling may be substituted for fresh apples. Pour filling into pie crust. Sprinkle with cinnamon and nutmeg and dot with butter. Follow directions above.

Quick Swiss Apple Pie

Pastry for 2-crust pie
1 can (21 ounces) cherry pie filling
1 can (21 ounces) apple pie filling
½ teaspoon cinnamon
¼ teaspoon nutmeg

Roll out bottom crust and line pie tin. Roll out top crust; set aside. In bottom of pie crust spoon cherries from cherry filling, leaving about ⅓ cup thickened juice in can. Gently spoon entire can of apple filling over cherries. Sprinkle with cinnamon and nutmeg. Moisten edge of pie crust with water. Add top crust and seal. Brush with milk and

sprinkle with sugar. Bake at 375 degrees for 35 to 45 minutes.

Cherry Pie

2½ tablespoons quick-cooking tapioca
⅛ teaspoon salt
1 cup sugar
6 drops red food coloring
3 cups drained water-packed red sour cherries
½ cup cherry juice
¼ teaspoon almond extract
Pastry for 9-inch 2-crust pie
1 tablespoon butter

Combine all ingredients except pastry and butter. Let stand about 15 minutes. Pour into pie shell; dot with butter. Cut air vents in top crust and place over filling; press top and bottom crusts together around edge. Crimp or flute. Bake at 375 degrees for about 50 minutes.

Cranberry Pie

2½ cups raw cranberries
1 cup water
1 cup sugar
4 tablespoons cornstarch
½ cup raisins
½ cup chopped walnuts
2 tablespoons butter
Baked 9-inch pie shell
1 cup whipping cream, whipped

In medium saucepan, cook cranberries in water until skins pop. Strain and save juice in pan. Mix sugar and cornstarch; add slowly to juice. Cook until thickened, stirring constantly. Stir in raisins, nuts, cooked cranberries, and butter. Pour into baked pie shell. Chill. Garnish with whipped cream. Makes 1 pie.

Very Berry Pie

1   bag (16 ounces, no sugar added) frozen
    boysenberries
1   bag (8 ounces, no sugar added) frozen
    blueberries
1   bag (8 ounces, no sugar added) frozen
    raspberries
1¾ cups sugar
½   teaspoon salt
½   cup cornstarch
    Pastry for two 2-crust pies

Thaw all berries; pour berries and all juice in mixing bowl. In separate bowl, mix sugar, salt, and cornstarch; pour on top of berries. Mix well with rubber spatula. Fill crusts, add top crusts, and bake at 375 degrees for 45 to 50 minutes or until golden brown. Makes 2 pies.

Very Berry Pie

Blueberry Pie

- 1 bag (16 ounces) frozen blueberries, thawed
- 1 cup sugar
- ¼ teaspoon salt
- 4 tablespoons cornstarch
  Pastry for 2-crust pie

Pour thawed berries and juice into large mixing bowl. In separate bowl, mix sugar, salt, and cornstarch; pour on top of berries. Mix well with rubber spatula. Fill crust, add top crust, and bake at 375 degrees for 45 to 50 minutes or until golden brown. Makes 1 pie.

Apricot Pineapple Pie

- 1 can (15¼ ounces) apricot halves
- 1 can (20 ounces) pineapple tidbits
- ¾ cup sugar
- ¼ cup plus 2 tablespoons cornstarch
- ¼ teaspoon salt
  Pastry for 2-crust pie

Drain ¼ cup apricot juice. Pour apricots and remaining juice in large mixing bowl. Cut apricots in half, making each piece ¼ of an apricot. Drain ½ cup pineapple juice. Add pineapple tidbits and remaining juice to apricots. In separate bowl, mix sugar, cornstarch, and salt; pour on top of fruit. Mix well with rubber spatula. Fill crust, add top crust, and bake at 375 degrees for 45 to 50 minutes or until golden brown. Makes 1 pie.

Rhubarb Pie

- 4 cups rhubarb (frozen, partially thawed)
- 1¾ cups sugar
- ¼ cup flour
- 2 tablespoons cornstarch
- ¼ teaspoon salt
- 1 egg
- 1 drop red food coloring
  Pastry for 2-crust pie

Place rhubarb in medium mixing bowl; let thaw 10 to 15 minutes. Drain liquid. In separate bowl, combine sugar, flour, cornstarch, and salt. Beat egg; blend with flour mixture. Add rhubarb and red food coloring; mix well. Pour into unbaked 9-inch pie shell. Roll out top crust; cut slits and place over filling. Seal; flute edges. Brush top with milk; sprinkle with sugar, if desired. Bake at 350 degrees for 45 minutes or until browned. Makes 1 pie.

Note: Four cups fresh rhubarb may be substituted for frozen rhubarb. Bake at 350 degrees for 50 to 55 minutes.

Quick Mincemeat Pie

- 1 jar (27 ounces) mincemeat
- 1 can (21 ounces) apple pie filling (cut apples in smaller pieces)
- ¾ cup nuts, chopped
  Pastry for two 2-crust pies
  Holiday Sauce (below)

Pour all filling ingredients into medium bowl and stir. Line two 9-inch pie tins with dough. Pour in filling; top with second crust. Seal and cut vent in the top. Brush top with half-and-half; sprinkle lightly with sugar. Bake at 375 degrees for 45 to 50 minutes. Serve with warm Holiday Sauce. Makes 2 pies.

Holiday Sauce

- ½ cup granulated sugar
- ½ cup brown sugar
- 2 tablespoons cornstarch
  Pinch salt
- 1 cup water
- 1 tablespoon butter
- ½ teaspoon imitation rum flavoring

In small saucepan, mix sugars, cornstarch, and salt until well blended. Add water and bring to boil, stirring constantly. Add butter and imitation rum flavoring. Makes about 1½ cups. Serve warm with mincemeat pie.

Raisin Pie

1½	cups raisins
1½	cups water
¼	cup pineapple juice, *or* ¼ cup more water
½	teaspoon vanilla
1	cup sugar
¼	cup cornstarch
½	teaspoon salt
¼	cup lemon juice
	Pastry for 8-inch 2-crust pie, rolled thin

In small saucepan, combine raisins, water, pineapple juice, and vanilla. Bring to boil and cook 5 minutes. Pour mixture through strainer. Set raisins aside, reserving liquid.

Mix sugar, cornstarch, and salt; add hot raisin liquid, beating with wire whip. Continue cooking and stirring until thick, about 5 minutes. Add raisins and lemon juice; pour into unbaked pie shell.

Roll out top crust and cut two 2-inch slits near center, then snip with scissors at sides and between slits, or make cut-out designs. Moisten edge of bottom crust. To adjust top crust, fold in half or roll loosely on rolling pin; center on filling. Pull slits apart slightly if necessary with knife, for steam to escape during baking. Trim top crust, allowing it to extend half an inch over rim. To seal, press top and bottom crusts together around rim. Fold edge of top crust under bottom crust; flute. Bake at 375 degrees for about 50 minutes or to the desired brownness.

Grasshopper Pie

1½	cups finely crushed chocolate wafers (25 wafers)
6	tablespoons butter or margarine, melted
6½	cups miniature marshmallows
½	cup milk
¼	cup crème de menthe syrup
1	cup whipping cream
	Few drops green food coloring (optional)
	Chocolate curls for garnish

Combine crushed wafers and melted butter. Spread evenly on bottom and sides of 9-inch pie

plate. Chill about 1 hour. In saucepan, combine marshmallows and milk. Cook over low heat until marshmallows are melted. Remove from heat and cool, stirring several times while cooling. Add crème de menthe. Whip cream and fold into marshmallow mixture. Add food coloring, if desired. Pour filling into chocolate crust. Garnish with whipped cream and chocolate curls.

Coconut Cream Pie

½	cup flaked coconut
	Unbaked 9-inch pie shell
3	eggs, slightly beaten
¼	cup sugar
¼	teaspoon cinnamon
¼	teaspoon nutmeg
¼	teaspoon vanilla
⅛	teaspoon salt
½	cup half-and-half
1¼	cups milk

Spread coconut evenly in bottom of unbaked pie shell; set aside. In separate bowl, beat eggs slightly; add sugar, cinnamon, nutmeg, vanilla, and salt. Mix well. Mix in half-and-half. Add milk and mix thoroughly. Pour over coconut and bake at 400 degrees for 50 to 55 minutes or until knife inserted comes out clean. May be served warm or chilled with whipped cream.

Buttermilk Pie

1½	cups sugar
1	cup buttermilk
½	cup Bisquick
⅓	cup margarine or butter, melted
1	teaspoon vanilla
3	eggs

Grease pie tin. Mix all ingredients and pour into pie tin. Bake at 350 degrees for about 30 minutes, or until knife inserted in center comes out clean. Cool five minutes. Serve warm or cold with fresh fruit or caramel sauce and whipped cream.

Coconut Cream Pie

Key Lime Pie

2 envelopes (2 tablespoons) unflavored
   gelatin
1 cup sugar
¼ teaspoon salt
6 egg yolks
¾ cup lime juice
½ cup water
1 teaspoon grated lime peel
  Few drops green food coloring
6 egg whites
¾ cup sugar
2 baked pie shells or graham cracker shells
  Whipped cream
  Lime, thinly sliced for garnish

Mix gelatin, 1 cup sugar, and salt. Beat egg yolks, lime juice, and water; pour into a saucepan. Add gelatin mixture; stir constantly over medium heat until mixture boils. Stir in lime peel and food coloring. Pour into bowl (do not leave in aluminum pan) and refrigerate until mixture mounds when dropped from spoon. Beat egg whites until soft peaks form. Gradually add ¾ cup sugar and continue beating until stiff. Fold into lime mixture. Pour into pie shells. Serve with whipped cream and garnish with thin slices of lime.

Lemon Cream Pie

1¼ cups sugar
¼ teaspoon salt
6 tablespoons cornstarch
1½ cups boiling water
3 eggs, slightly beaten
6 tablespoons lemon juice
¼ teaspoon grated lemon rind
2 tablespoons butter or margarine
  Baked 9-inch pie shell
1 cup heavy cream, whipped and
  sweetened

In 2- or 3-quart saucepan, combine sugar, salt, and cornstarch; blend well. Place over medium heat and add boiling water, stirring rapidly until smooth and thick. Bring to full boil to thoroughly cook cornstarch; remove from heat. In medium

bowl, beat eggs slightly. Add small amount of hot pudding to eggs while stirring rapidly. Return egg mixture to hot pudding in saucepan and reheat, stirring constantly, just until smooth. Remove from heat; add lemon juice and rind and butter. Pour into baked pie shell. Cover surface with plastic wrap to prevent skin from forming. Chill. Served topped with whipped cream.

Lemon Meringue Pie

Follow directions for Lemon Cream Pie, *except* separate eggs, using only yolks in filling. Beat whites on high speed of electric mixer, adding 6 tablespoons sugar gradually. Continue beating until mixture stands in stiff peaks. Pile on hot filling; seal well to edge of pie crust. Bake at 375 degrees for about 15 minutes or until delicately browned. Cool thoroughly, at least 4 hours.

Baked Alaska Pie

1 8-inch baked pie shell
1 quart peppermint ice cream
2 to 3 tablespoons chocolate syrup
5 egg whites
1 teaspoon vanilla
½ teaspoon cream of tartar
⅔ cup sugar

Spoon ice cream into pie shell. Drizzle with chocolate syrup or fudge sauce. Place in freezer until ready to use.

Heat oven to 500 degrees. Beat egg whites, vanilla, and cream of tartar until foamy. Gradually beat in sugar until mixture is stiff and glossy. Completely cover ice cream in pie shell with meringue, sealing well to edge of crust and piling high. (If desired, pie may be frozen up to 24 hours at this point.) When ready to serve, bake pie on lowest oven rack for 3 to 5 minutes or until meringue is light brown. Serve immediately. Or return to freezer until ready to serve. Makes 6 to 8 servings.

Baked Alaska Pie

Fresh Strawberry Pie

3	cups water
1	cup sugar
1	small package (3 ounces) strawberry gelatin
3	tablespoons cornstarch
3	cups fresh strawberries, washed and hulled
1	baked pie shell

In medium saucepan, bring water and sugar to boil. Mix gelatin with cornstarch; gradually add to boiling mixture. Cook over medium-high heat, stirring constantly, for 5 minutes or until mixture is clear and slightly thickened. Let stand at room temperature until just warm, about 15 minutes. While mixture is cooling, wash and hull strawberries. Place berries in large mixing bowl. Pour gelatin mixture over strawberries and gently fold together. Mound in baked pie shell. Chill for at least 1 hour before serving. Top with low-fat whipped topping, if desired. Makes 8 servings.

Cream Pie

Basic Cream Pie

1	quart milk
2	cups half-and-half
2	tablespoons butter
¾	cup sugar
3	egg yolks
½	cup sugar
¼	teaspoon salt
½	cup cornstarch
1½	teaspoons vanilla
2	baked 9-inch pie shells
	Whipped cream

Reserve up to 1 cup milk to mix with cornstarch. Place remaining milk in top of double boiler; add half-and-half, butter, and ¾ cup sugar. Cook until butter is melted and milk is scalded.

In bowl, whisk egg yolks well; add ½ cup sugar and salt and whisk very well. Slowly add egg mixture to hot milk mixture, stirring constantly for about half a minute, and allow to cook for 15 to 20 minutes. (This gives eggs time to cook and start thickening. Undercooking at this point slows the finishing process by as much as half an hour.)

Mix reserved milk and cornstarch; slowly add to hot mixture. Stir constantly or lumps will form. Continue to stir for at least 2 minutes, then every 5 minutes for 15 to 20 minutes. When pudding is thick, stir in vanilla. Remove double boiler from stove. Pour filling into pie shells, rounding tops of pies. When cool, top with whipped cream. Makes 2 pies.

Coconut Cream Pie

Add ½ cup coconut (toasted, if desired) to pie filling. Pour into baked shell. Chill 3 to 4 hours. When ready to serve, whip cream and spread over pie. Top with another ½ cup coconut.

Banana Cream Pie

Slice 2 bananas into pie shell. Pour filling over bananas. Chill 3 to 4 hours. When ready to serve, whip cream and spread over pie.

Chocolate Cream Pie

Add ½ to ⅔ cups semisweet chocolate chips to hot pudding. Stir until melted. Pour into pie shell. Chill 3 to 4 hours. When ready to serve, whip cream and spread over pie. Makes 6 servings.

Pralines and Cream Pie

Add ½ cup caramel sauce (ice cream topping) and ½ cup chopped pecans to basic filling. Pour into baked shell. Chill 3 to 4 hours. Top with sweetened whipped cream before serving.

German Chocolate Pie

To filling add ¾ cup semisweet chocolate chips, ½ cup coconut, ¼ cup chopped pecans, and ¼ cup caramel sauce (ice cream topping). Stir until well blended. Pour into baked pie crust.

Tropical Isle Pie

To filling add ½ cup coconut, ⅓ cup drained, crushed pineapple, and ⅓ cup drained mandarin oranges. Pour into baked pie crust.

Butterscotch Cream Pie

1⅓	cups sugar
2½	cups milk
¾	cup cream
5	tablespoons cornstarch
¼	teaspoon salt
3	egg yolks
1	teaspoon vanilla
2	tablespoons butter or margarine
	Baked 9-inch pie crust
1	cup whipping cream
¼	cup chopped nuts, if desired

Measure sugar into heavy saucepan or skillet. Stir constantly over high heat until sugar is nearly melted. Reduce heat to medium and continue stirring until all sugar is melted and turns a light amber color. In the meantime, heat milk; stir hot milk into melted sugar cautiously. Sugar will bubble and steam, then harden. On low heat, stir mixture occasionally until sugar is completely dissolved in milk.

Gradually add table cream to cornstarch to make a smooth paste. Stir into hot milk mixture; cook and stir until mixture forms a smooth, thick pudding. Boil a minute or two, stirring vigorously, then remove from heat. Add salt to egg yolks; stir in some of the hot pudding. Stir egg mixture back into pudding and cook another 2 to 3 minutes. Remove from heat; add vanilla and butter. Cook 5 minutes. Pour into baked pie shell. Chill 3 to 4 hours. When ready to serve, whip cream and spread over pie. Sprinkle with nuts. Makes 6 servings.

Note: Two whole eggs may be used, but filling may not be as smooth.

Pumpkin Pie

- 1½ cups pumpkin
- ½ teaspoon cinnamon
- ½ teaspoon nutmeg
- ¼ teaspoon ginger
- ¼ teaspoon allspice
- ½ cup granulated sugar
- ⅓ cup brown sugar
- 1 teaspoon salt
- 1½ tablespoons cornstarch
- 2 eggs
- 1 cup evaporated milk
- 1 cup water
  Pastry for 1-crust pie
  Whipped cream, if desired

Place pumpkin in large mixing bowl. In separate bowl, mix cinnamon, nutmeg, ginger, allspice, granulated sugar, brown sugar, salt, and cornstarch. Add to pumpkin and mix until blended. Add eggs and evaporated milk and mix until blended. Add water and mix well. Pour into unbaked pie shell and bake at 375 degrees for 50 to 60 minutes or until knife inserted in center comes out clean. Top with whipped cream, if desired. Makes 1 pie.

Five-Step Black Bottom Pie

- 36 gingersnaps
- ½ cup melted butter or margarine
  Dash salt
- 4 cups milk
- 4 tablespoons butter or margarine
- ½ cup cornstarch
- 1½ cups sugar
- 4 egg yolks, slightly beaten
- 2 teaspoons vanilla
- 2 squares baking chocolate
- 2 envelopes (2 tablespoons) unflavored gelatin
- ½ cup cold water
- 4 egg whites, beaten stiff
- 1 cup sugar
- 1 teaspoon cream of tartar
- 2 teaspoons imitation rum flavoring
- 1 cup whipped cream, sweetened if desired

Step 1: Crush gingersnaps; roll fine and combine with ½ cup melted butter or margarine and salt. Mold evenly into 11-inch springform pan. Prepare filling.

Step 2: Scald milk; add 4 tablespoons butter. Combine cornstarch and sugar; moisten with enough water to make a paste. Stir paste into scalded milk and cook until mixture comes to a boil, stirring constantly. Stir hot mixture gradually into slightly beaten egg yolks. Return to heat and cook 2 minutes. Add vanilla. Remove 2 cups of custard; add chocolate and beat well. Pour into crumb crust and chill.

Step 3: Blend gelatin with cold water; set a few minutes, then fold into remaining hot custard. Cool.

Step 4: Beat egg whites, 1 cup sugar, and cream of tartar into a meringue. Add rum flavoring and fold into custard from step 2.

Step 5: When chocolate custard has set, pour plain custard on top and chill until set. Serve with whipped cream and bits of chocolate for decoration.

Puff Pastries

- 1 cup flour
- ¼ teaspoon salt
- ½ cup butter (or ¼ cup shortening and ¼ cup butter)
- 1 cup boiling water
- 4 eggs

Sift flour with salt. Combine butter and boiling water in saucepan; cook on low heat until butter is melted. Add flour all at once and stir vigorously until mixture forms a ball and leaves sides of pan. Cook about 2 minutes until mixture is very dry. Remove from heat. Add unbeaten eggs one at a time, beating well after each addition. Continue beating until a thick dough forms. For cream puffs, drop by tablespoonfuls onto brown-paper-lined baking sheet, about 2 inches apart. (See variations below for other baking directions.) Bake at 425 degrees about 15 minutes. Reduce heat to 375 degrees and bake for 15 more minutes. Bake about 30 to 40 minutes total, or until beads of moisture no longer appear on surface. Do not open oven door during early part of baking. Remove to wire racks to cool. When cool, cut slit in side of each puff; remove doughy centers, if necessary. Makes about 12 large cream puff shells.

Cream Puffs

Fill with cream filling made from pudding and pie filling mix, following package directions; or fill with sweetened whipped cream or any other favorite cream filling.

Eclairs

Onto paper-lined baking sheets, force dough through decorating tube in strips about 1 inch wide and 4 inches long. Bake about 25 minutes. Fill as for cream puffs. Frost with chocolate powdered sugar frosting. Makes about 18 eclairs.

Cocktail Puffs

Drop dough by small teaspoonfuls onto paper-lined baking sheets. Bake 17 to 20 minutes. Fill with any savory filling. (See Ribbon Sandwich fillings, for example.) Makes 4 to 5 dozen small puffs.

Puff Shells

Drop dough from tablespoon into deep hot fat (375 degrees). Fry 10 to 15 seconds or until a good crust forms, turning often. Drain well, then cut top off each shell. Fill hot shells with creamed fish, poultry, meat, eggs, or vegetables. Or cool shells and fill with a salad mixture. Replace tops before serving. Makes about 12 large shells.

Chocolate Party Puffs

- 1 recipe cocktail puffs (makes 60 puffs)
- 1 quart vanilla ice cream
- 1 quart heavy cream, whipped
- 1 tablespoon sugar, or to taste
- 1 teaspoon vanilla, or to taste
- 1 cup chocolate syrup
- 1 jar (16 ounces) maraschino cherries, well drained

Slit cooled puffs and pull out any dough strands inside. Fill shells with vanilla ice cream. Freeze on tray in single layer. Pack in plastic bags and store in freezer until ready to use.

To assemble, whip cream; add sugar, vanilla, and syrup. Fold slightly thawed puffs and cherries into cream. Serve immediately from a glass bowl. Makes 20 servings of 3 puffs each, or 15 servings of 4 puffs each.

Apple Crisp

Topping

  1 cup butter, cold
  1 cup brown sugar
  1 cup flour
  1 cup oatmeal
  ¼ teaspoon baking powder

In a large bowl, mix butter, brown sugar, flour, oatmeal, and baking powder just until butter is broken up and ingredients are mixed. Mixture should be crumbly. Set aside.

Filling

  6 cups canned apples or 6 to 8 fresh apples, peeled and sliced
  ½ cup sugar
  ¼ teaspoon salt
  1 teaspoon cinnamon

Place apples in 9x13-inch pan. Sprinkle with sugar, salt, and cinnamon. Crumble crisp topping on top. Bake at 350 degrees for 25 to 35 minutes or until golden brown. (If fresh apples are used, bake 45 minutes.) Serve warm or cold, with whipped cream or ice cream. Makes 12 to 15 servings.

Pumpkin Spice Dessert

Crust

  1 cup prepared biscuit mix
  ½ cup quick rolled oats
  ½ cup brown sugar
  ¼ cup margarine

Mix biscuit mix, rolled oats, brown sugar, and margarine until crumbly. Press into a 9x13-inch pan. Bake at 375 degrees for 10 minutes.

Middle Layer

  1 can (16 ounces) pumpkin
  1 tall can evaporated milk
  2 eggs
  ¾ cup sugar
  ½ teaspoon salt
  1 teaspoon cinnamon
  ½ teaspoon ginger
  ¼ teaspoon cloves

Beat pumpkin, milk, eggs, sugar, salt, and spices until well mixed. Pour over crust. Return to oven and bake 25 minutes longer.

Topping

  ½ cup pecans, chopped
  ½ cup brown sugar
  2 tablespoons butter
    Whipped cream

Mix chopped pecans, brown sugar, and butter until crumbly. Sprinkle over pudding. Return to oven and bake 15 to 20 minutes longer. Cool. Serve with whipped cream. Makes 24 servings.

Caramel Dumplings in Sauce

Caramel Sauce

  1½ cups sugar (divided)
  2 cups hot water
  2 tablespoons butter
  ⅛ teaspoon salt

Caramelize ¾ cup sugar in heavy skillet over medium heat. Add hot water and cover until bubbling subsides. Add remaining ¾ cup sugar, butter, and salt. Cook until smooth.

Dumplings

  2 cups flour
  2 teaspoons baking powder
  5 tablespoons shortening
  ¼ teaspoon salt
  ¾ cup milk
  1 teaspoon vanilla

Mix dough. Drop by tablespoonfuls into hot caramel sauce. Leave space between dumplings. Cook on medium heat 30 minutes with lid on. Serve warm with ice cream or whipped cream.

Note: Two cups Bisquick may be used in place of dry ingredients.

Apple Crisp

Apple Dumplings

1 quart (about 4 medium) cooking apples,
   pared, cored, sliced
2 tablespoons sugar
2 tablespoons water
1 tablespoon lemon juice
   Dough (to right)
   Sauce (next page)
   Vanilla Sauce (next page)

Mix ingredients well and place in 8x8-inch baking
pan. Cover pan with aluminum foil and bake at
350 degrees for 10 to 15 minutes while preparing
dough. Remove apples from oven and cover with
dough. Cut steam vents in dough. Pour sauce over
dough. Return to oven and bake 30 minutes more,
or until brown. Serve warm with hot Vanilla
Sauce. Makes 9 servings.

Dough
1½ cups flour
¼ cup sugar
¼ teaspoon salt
2 teaspoons baking powder
½ cup vegetable shortening
1 egg, slightly beaten
⅓ cup milk

Sift dry ingredients. Cut in shortening as for pie
crust, until mixture resembles coarse meal.

Combine egg and milk; stir into dry ingredients. Combine thoroughly; knead on lightly floured board 20 times. Pat and roll out to about ½-inch thickness. Carefully place over apples. Trim excess, if necessary, so that dough fits pan.

Sauce

- ½ cup brown sugar
- ⅓ cup water
- 1 tablespoon butter or margarine
  Cinnamon

Combine brown sugar, water, and butter. Boil until sugar is dissolved. Pour over dough. Sprinkle lightly with cinnamon.

Vanilla Sauce

- 2 tablespoons flour
- 2 tablespoons sugar
- ⅛ teaspoon salt
- ¾ cup hot water
  Small can (¾ cup) evaporated milk
- ½ teaspoon vanilla
- 2 tablespoons butter or margarine

Combine dry ingredients. Stir in hot water and bring mixture to boil, stirring constantly. Add evaporated milk, vanilla, and butter; reheat. Makes about 1½ cups.

Steamed Carrot Pudding

- 1 cup carrots, grated
- ¾ cup raw potatoes, grated
- ½ cup apples, grated (with or without peel)
- ½ cup butter
- 1 cup raisins
- ½ cup walnuts or pecans
- 1 cup sugar
- 1 cup flour
- 1 teaspoon cinnamon
- ½ teaspoon allspice
- ½ teaspoon cloves
- ½ teaspoon nutmeg
- ½ teaspoon salt
- 1 teaspoon baking soda
  Lemon Sauce (below)

In mixing bowl, combine carrots, potatoes, apples, butter, raisins, and nuts; mix with spoon until

blended. In separate bowl, mix sugar, flour, cinnamon, allspice, cloves, nutmeg, salt, and baking soda. Add flour mixture to carrot mixture; stir until blended. (It will form a stiff, gooey mixture.) Place mixture in clean, greased number 2 can or ovenproof bowl of about the same size. Do not fill container more than ¾ full. Cover container with foil. Steam pudding or cook in pressure cooker.

To pressure cook: Place rack in bottom of cooker to keep pudding from touching bottom of pan. Add about ¾ inch water; set container of pudding in cooker. Cook 20 minutes with steam valve open, and an additional 50 minutes with valve closed.

To steam: Place container of pudding in pot tall enough to fit container and still have a tight lid. Add about 1 inch water. Place lid on tightly and cook for 2½ hours.

Pudding may be made ahead of time and stored in refrigerator. Warm in oven or microwave before serving. Serve topped with Lemon Sauce.

Lemon Sauce

- 1 cup sugar
- 2 tablespoons cornstarch
- 2 cups cool water
- ¼ cup lemon juice
- 2 tablespoons butter

In saucepan, combine sugar, cornstarch, and water. Heat to boiling, stirring constantly. Add lemon juice and butter.

Jiffy Lemon Sauce

- ½ cup sugar
- 2 tablespoons cornstarch
- ⅛ teaspoon salt
- 1 cup water
- 1 teaspoon grated lemon rind
- 4 tablespoons lemon juice
- 2 tablespoons butter

Mix sugar, cornstarch, and salt with ¼ cup water. Add remaining water and bring to boil. Remove from heat and add remaining ingredients. Cool slightly. Makes 1¾ cups, or about 14 servings of 2 tablespoons each.

Chocolate Pudding Dessert

- 1½ cups flour
- 1½ cubes (¾ cup) butter
- ⅔ cup chopped nuts
- 1 cup powdered sugar
- 1 package (8 ounces) softened cream cheese
- 1 carton (9 ounces) frozen whipped topping
- 2 packages (3 ounces each) instant chocolate pudding mix
- 3 cups milk

Combine flour, butter, and nuts; cut together as for pie crust, until mixture resembles coarse meal. Press well into 9x13-inch baking pan. Bake at 325 degrees for 30 minutes. Remove from oven and cool. Beat together powdered sugar and cream cheese until fluffy. Add half the whipped topping. Spread on cooled crust.

Prepare pudding according to package directions, using just 3 cups milk. Spread pudding on cream cheese layer. Spread remaining whipped topping on pudding layer. Sprinkle with additional chopped nuts, if desired. Chill several hours or overnight. Makes 15 servings.

Note: Butterscotch or other instant pudding flavors may be used.

Rice Pudding

- 2 cups milk
- 1 small can (5⅓ ounces) evaporated milk
- ½ cup plus 2 tablespoons sugar
- 2 eggs, slightly beaten
- ¼ teaspoon salt
- 1 tablespoon cornstarch
- 2 cups cooked rice
- ½ cup raisins
- ⅛ teaspoon nutmeg
- ⅛ teaspoon cinnamon
- 1 teaspoon vanilla

Place 1½ cups milk plus evaporated milk and 6 tablespoons sugar in top of double boiler. Heat until milk is scalded. In mixing bowl, whisk eggs; add salt and remaining 4 tablespoons sugar and whisk again. Slowly pour egg mixture into scalded milk, stirring constantly with wire whisk. Cook 15 to 20 minutes, stirring occasionally. In small bowl, mix reserved ½ cup milk and cornstarch together; slowly pour into milk mixture, stirring constantly until pudding begins to thicken. (Stir constantly or lumps will form.) Stir thoroughly and cook 10 to 15 more minutes or until cornstarch flavor is gone. Add cooked rice and cook 7 more minutes. Remove from heat and add raisins, nutmeg, cinnamon, and vanilla. Serves 8.

Note: If double boiler is not available, place stainless steel bowl on top of small saucepan of boiling water, or cook pudding in saucepan, stirring constantly. (Cooking time will be less in saucepan.)

Sago Pudding

- 1 cup sago (old-fashioned large tapioca)
- 3 cups water
- 2 or 3 apples, peeled and sliced
- ⅔ cup sugar
- Pinch salt
- Hard Sauce (below)

Soak sago in water for a few minutes. Add apples, sugar, and salt. Bake at 325 degrees about 1 hour. Serve with hard sauce, nutmeg, and thin cream.

Hard Sauce

- 4 tablespoons butter or margarine
- 1 cup powdered sugar
- 1 teaspoon boiling water
- Few grains salt
- 1 teaspoon vanilla

Cream butter and sugar. Add remaining ingredients; beat until smooth and fluffy. Makes about 1 cup. Sauce may be stored indefinitely in refrigerator. If sauce becomes dry, add a few drops boiling water and reheat.

Rice Pudding

Creamy Tapioca Pudding

3	tablespoons quick-cooking tapioca
3	tablespoons sugar
⅛	teaspoon salt
2	cups milk
1	egg, separated
2	tablespoons sugar
¾	teaspoon vanilla

In small saucepan, mix tapioca, sugar, salt, milk, and egg yolk. Let stand while preparing meringue. Beat egg white until foamy. Add 2 tablespoons sugar and beat until soft peaks form. Let stand while cooking pudding.

Cook tapioca mixture over medium heat to full boil, stirring constantly (6 to 8 minutes). Gradually pour hot mixture into beaten egg white, stirring quickly to blend. Stir in vanilla; cool slightly. Stir. Serve warm or chilled, garnish as desired. Makes 5 servings.

Baked Custard

4	eggs, lightly beaten
2¾	cups milk
½	cup table cream
½	cup sugar
½	teaspoon salt
¾	teaspoon vanilla
	Nutmeg (optional)

Beat eggs; add milk, cream, sugar, salt, and vanilla. Strain into individual custard cups set in pan of hot water. Sprinkle nutmeg on custard, if desired. Bake at 350 degrees for 40 to 50 minutes. Custard is cooked when knife inserted near center comes out clean. Remove from water to cool. Chill and serve in cups. Makes 6 to 8 servings.

Note: Custard may be baked in 1½- or 2-quart casserole instead of individual cups.

Bread Pudding

10	slices bread*
	About 1 cube butter, melted
¾ to 1	cup raisins
6	eggs
6	cups milk
¾	cup sugar
	Pinch salt
¾	teaspoon vanilla
¾	teaspoon plus dash nutmeg
	Lemon Butter Sauce (below)

Spray 9x13-inch pan with nonstick cooking spray; set aside. Cut off crusts. Place one layer of bread slices in pan and brush with melted butter. Sprinkle raisins on top. Place another layer of bread on top of raisins and brush with melted butter.

In large bowl, mix eggs, milk, sugar, salt, vanilla, and ¾ teaspoon nutmeg with wire whisk. Pour over bread. Sprinkle nutmeg over top of pudding and allow to set for 30 to 45 minutes. Bake at 350 degrees for 45 minutes or until custard is formed and knife inserted comes out clean. Serve with Lemon Butter Sauce. Serves 16.

* Stale bread may be used for Bread Pudding.

Lemon Butter Sauce

2	cups sugar
¼	cup plus ½ teaspoon cornstarch
¼	teaspoon salt
2	cups water
1	cup butter, cut in small pieces
1½	teaspoons lemon extract

Place sugar, cornstarch, and salt in 4-quart saucepan; stir until blended. Add water. Bring to a boil; cook for 5 minutes, stirring constantly. Remove from heat; stir in butter and lemon extract until butter is melted and mixture is creamy. Pour small amount on each piece of bread pudding. Makes 4 cups.

Note: This delicious sauce may be used on other puddings and cakes.

Frozen Fruit Dessert

1   gallon pineapple sherbet, softened
3   packages (10 ounces each) frozen rasp-
      berries, thawed
5   bananas, cubed

Fold ingredients together. Put into covered plastic containers and freeze. Dessert may be made ahead of time and stored in freezer. Makes 35 servings.

Note: You can also use equal parts pineapple sherbet and vanilla ice cream, softened.

Rhubarb Whip

1   pound (4 cups) rhubarb, cut in 1-inch
      pieces
½   cup sugar
¼   cup water
1   package (3 ounces) strawberry gelatin
½   cup cold water
½   cup whipping cream, whipped
      Fresh strawberries (optional)

Combine rhubarb, sugar, and water; bring to boil. Cover and cook on low heat 8 to 10 minutes. Remove from heat; add gelatin and stir until gelatin dissolves (about 2 minutes). Stir in cold water; chill until partially set. Whip until fluffy. Fold in whipped cream and pour into sherbet glasses. Chill. Garnish with fresh strawberries and additional whipped cream, if desired. Makes about 8 half-cup servings.

Nutmeg-Pineapple Marshmallow Squares

24   large marshmallows, cut in squares
1¾   cups milk
⅛   teaspoon salt
½   envelope (½ tablespoon) unflavored
      gelatin
¼   cup cold milk
1   cup heavy cream, whipped
½   teaspoon ground nutmeg
¼   teaspoon grated lemon rind
1   cup (8 ounces) crushed pineapple,
      drained
½   cup graham cracker crumbs

Place marshmallows, milk, and salt in top of double boiler. Heat over hot water until marshmallows are melted. In the meantime, soften gelatin in ¼ cup cold milk, then stir into melted marshmallow mixture. Cool until mixture begins to thicken. Fold in whipped cream, nutmeg, lemon rind, and pineapple.

Press 4 tablespoons graham cracker crumbs in bottom of greased 9x9-inch pan. Gently spoon in marshmallow mixture; top with remaining graham cracker crumbs. Chill overnight or several hours in refrigerator. Cut into squares and serve. Makes 9 servings.

Lion House Cheese Ball

Index